COOKING WITH LOVE

HENRY HOLT AND COMPANY

NEW YORK

COOKING
WITH

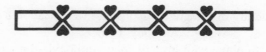

LOVE

by

Francis Anthony

Library of Congress Cataloging-in-Publication Data
Anthony, Francis.
Cooking with love/[Francis Anthony].—1st ed.
p. cm.
ISBN 0-8050-1191-9
1. Cookery. I. Title.
TX714.A57 1990
641.5—dc20   89-15580
CIP

Henry Holt books are available at special discounts
for bulk purchases for sales promotions, premiums,
fund-raising, or educational use. Special editions
or book excerpts can also be created to specification.
For details contact:
Special Sales Director
Henry Holt and Company, Inc.
115 West 18th Street
New York, New York 10011

First Edition

Book Design by Claire M. Naylon
Printed in the United States of America
1 3 5 7 9 10 8 6 4 2

To the original creators
of cooking with love,
my mother and father.

Contents

Introduction

Cooking with love is . . .

- Treating yourself and your body with love and respect; selecting and preparing foods that will please the senses, nourish the body, and satisfy the soul.
- Appreciating the special qualities of special foods, so that the whole vast and wonderful range of raw materials in your market and greengrocer's is available to you; so that never again will you stare uncomprehendingly at an eggplant or cook a luscious roast beef to death.
- Learning to serve guests in your home with style and panache and the kind of simple elegance that attends good food, beautifully prepared, and joyously served, so that an invitation to dine is a call to celebration.

Introduction

And above all, it is having *fun* in the kitchen!

Cooking with love means never having to feel chained to your stove, never feeling that getting dinner on the table is a teeth-gritting experience rather than a charming interlude. Food is sensuous. Squeeze tomatoes between your fingers, toss salad with your hands, feel the texture of spices. Put a loving touch in every dish and don't be afraid to make mistakes, because life is full of them. Make mistakes; eat your mistakes; then cook some more.

I call myself the Love Chef because I love food, I love to cook, and I love people.

COOKING WITH LOVE

I.

Cooking
with Love
in Your Own
Kitchen

PRESENTATION

Before getting to the recipes, I want to talk about ambience. It is as important a part of the dining experience as the food you eat, because the sights and sounds and feelings around your table contribute equally to making dinner just what you want it to be—calm and restful, or romantic and exciting, or giddy and fun. Even before you turn on the oven, turn on the eyes! Make the presentation of your meal as attractive as it can be. Here's what I like on a dinner table.

Dishes

For your one basic set, nothing can beat plain white or soft beige dishes. They create the most handsome background for your foods and, depending on the rest of the table setting, can look informal or extremely elegant. Keep the plates simple and let the food itself be your design. If you are someone who enjoys shopping for dinnerware and your budget can stand it, it's fun to have a variety of place settings for two—

maybe bright country-French style, maybe rustic brown plates. Don't let your "good" china collect dust on an inaccessible shelf in the cupboard. Keep two place settings down on the easy-to-reach shelves and bring them out to use now and then to give your spirits a lift.

Napkins

If you have some of those old-fashioned, oversized linen napkins that your grandmother gave you, use them for special dinners for two. There is something about a very big, very soft white linen dinner napkin that makes any meal seem classy. But always use cloth napkins! Buy cotton ones in a variety of colors and vary them with the seasons or to suit your table setting or mood. Cloth napkins are infinitely nicer than paper and they're easy to wash.

Candles

Lots of white candles add a special feeling to any meal. I like both tall ones in candle holders and the short, stubby kind that sit in low glass containers and can be massed around for a dramatic effect. Never make the mistake of thinking candles are for dressy occasions only; candles are for every day.

Placemats

Placemats are another inexpensive, simple way to give a table a little style and polish. Simple straw mats look great on butcher-block kitchen tables; mirrored glass mats look really special for a command-performance dinner.

Flowers

I love them on a dinner table, or anywhere! Put a big bunch of daisies in a chunky earthenware pot. Put a single iris or daffodil in a clear, thin vase. Buy some potted geraniums and put them on the table or around the area where you'll be eating. Flowers and greens look great hooked on a pegboard or on adjacent counters. The centerpiece doesn't have to be flowers at all. A bunch of gourds, small melons, or dried artichokes sitting right on the table or in straw baskets gives a bright, cheery look to any meal.

Candlelight, a pretty and colorful table, fresh flowers—all these are a way of saying I love you, a way of treating the eye as well as the taste buds, of making a meal an entertainment.

Speaking of tables, you don't *have* to eat at the official dining table. Maybe the evening you are planning suggests buffet-style dishes served up in the kitchen, or plates brought out to a low coffee table in front of the living-room couch for cozy and casual ambience. Maybe your guest is a football freak and you're planning a Monday-night-in-front-of-the-TV kind of dinner. Then you might set up trays or small tables in the TV room, or clear the desk. Another nice dinner might utilize an electric wok—a wonderful appliance that's not at all hard to use—bring it into the bedroom or out on your terrace. Look around your space with an open mind and don't be afraid to think in terms of a movable feast.

Hardworking, two-career couples need special loving

care at night. Let dinner be a time to relax, unwind, and switch from the mental pressures of a busy day to the sensual delights of dinner for two. Unhook the phone, light a candle or two, leave a love note under your mate's dinner plate, and design a meal to fit the day. Maybe one partner had a heavy business lunch; then it's time for a light and easy dinner, maybe a fresh spinach salad or a mushroom omelette. If your partner has been traveling and is getting back home for the first time in a day or two or more, it's time to plan something slow and elegant.

A word about menu planning. As I say over and over: A cookbook isn't a bible, it's just a guide to look to for suggestions and ideas, information and inspiration. Use cookbooks as your guides and then adapt. Ten people cooking the same recipe will turn out ten different dishes, each taking on a little of the personality of the cook creating it and varying with the quality of the ingredients, the way your particular oven works, et cetera. The same holds true for planning a menu.

A well-planned meal should be orchestrated, not contrived. Decide first on a main course and let your complementary courses build on it. The entrée is the focal point and usually the heartiest or most substantial part of the meal, and its taste should dominate. Keep soups or other first courses lighter than the entrée and think of accompanying vegetables in terms of how attractive they will look, as well as how well they will complement the centerpiece dish. Avoid one-color meals and meals composed of elements that are all soft and mushy or hard and crunchy. Strive for balance, variety, and interest.

KITCHEN SETUP

Your kitchen should be a comfy work center that will make you happy. Bring in a television or radio so you can watch or listen to your favorite show or tape; fill the walls with framed posters, pictures, and love letters; put in a wall phone with a long cord. Don't hide pots and pans on high shelves; hang them or keep them in bottom cabinets. Pegboards and hooks work wonders even in the smallest galley kitchens. The more equipment you have out and available, the more fun you will have cooking.

Shelves of attractive glass or plastic canisters filled with herbs, spices, pastas of many shapes, and other dry foods give an uncluttered look and are ready and at hand when something is needed quickly. Also, the different shapes and textures of the food create an attractive appearance.

An added benefit for a wall display is the space it will leave you in your cabinets. Store those items not often used, such as large platters, large mixing bowls, baking pans, and other odd-sized items. Dishes, glassware, condiments, and grocery goods should be convenient.

The lighting should be comfortable. I love dimmers in the kitchen to change the mood; a soft light is so much more appealing than a glaring bright one. A counter light over your work area is also very important.

If you have a large kitchen, a good work center is a must. It will quickly turn into a talk center, a quick-bite center, a drying-tears center, and a chatting-on-the-phone center.

Even a smaller kitchen should have a rolling butcher block or table that can be used for other things. Throw a tablecloth over it and it becomes a great serving cart, an extra table for parties, or a dinner table in front of the TV. It also makes a versatile buffet table and a convenient bar for parties; the bottom can hold tubs of ice and beer and can be easily rolled from the kitchen into the "action" and back again for refilling. The top is great for liquor and fixings.

COOKWARE

A good set of everyday cookware is a wise investment. Avoid dime-store-variety pots and pans. I prefer *heavy* stainless steel in a variety of sizes for ease in the cleanup process. The timing directions I give in the following recipes work for my pots. You may find a slight difference with your own cookware, so you should adjust times accordingly. Remember, if you have to face a battery of hard-to-clean pots and pans every night, you'll soon dislike being in the kitchen.

Of course, sharing the cleanup chores with someone else is a blessing, and the time can be used to chat or watch TV at the same time.

TOOLS AND GADGETS

Everyone would like to have a fully equipped kitchen, but the primary tools you'll need to prepare your everyday meals are a good large (12- to 14-inch) chef's knife, plastic cutting board, wooden spoons, and a good set of cookware. It is great to have a food processor, but a basic kitchen can get along fine without one for everyday meals.

Choosing your basic chef's knife is one of your most

important kitchen decisions. You can recognize a good knife when you see that the blade continues into the handle and is embedded in it. Hold the knife in your hand; it should feel comfortable and well balanced. In addition to this basic knife, you will need slicing, carving, and paring knives, and a vegetable peeler.

Wooden cutting boards have no place in my kitchen other than as trays or bread boards. Plastic cutting boards come in numerous sizes and can be easily sanitized, making bacteria less of a problem.

I love wooden spoons, lots of them, in all sizes, because they are great for stirring and scraping. The one you've seen me use on television is Mom's, with the original crack from the time my brother said something she didn't like.

Always remember when buying a particular gadget to look for durability and ease of cleaning. Sure, you'll collect all kinds of things, but buy what you'll really use from time to time to reduce your kitchen work. If you are near a town that has a restaurant-supply house, it would make sense to poke around and see what you can add to your collection. Flea markets and garage sales are good sources for everyday items as well as unusual serving pieces. When I was putting together my cooking school in 1973, I remember finding dozens of unusual trays and serving pieces all in one afternoon at a large flea market in Edison, New Jersey.

Collect baskets to use as food holders; they make a great presentation. If you have the room, hang them in your kitchen. They create visual excitement and are then easily available. One Christmas I had to pick up some visiting aunts at Radio City Music Hall in Manhattan. At the last minute, I grabbed one of my large baskets, threw red and green napkins on the bottom along with glass cups, apple-cinnamon shortbread cookies, and a large jar of my spiked eggnog. I drove them all over the city to see the Christmas windows and lights of holiday New York. They are still talking about my "pretty basket" presentation.

SPICES AND HERBS

Spices and herbs should be stored in a cool, dry area away from heat and direct sun. Purchase spices in small quantities to ensure their flavor will be alive and vibrant when added to recipes. You might start a spice-sharing club with friends so all can enjoy a steady and assorted collection of aromatics. It's fun to experiment and taste the creative employment of herbs and spices. For instance, coriander sprinkled on fresh corn on the cob highlights its sweetness and you will be able to forget the salt shaker. See the section on "Seasonal Cooking" for more ways to complement vegetables with herbs and spices.

I like to keep a couple of pots of my favorite herbs on the windowsill, not only to add green to the environment but so that they are readily available to use for cooking and garnishing. Mom and Dad grow basil and keep me, and many of my friends, supplied with this fragrant herb. I never seem to have enough of it, partly because of my ravenous appetite for pesto, that heavenly basic sauce that I dab on broiled fish, steak, chops, chicken, pizza, bread, and pasta (see page 59).

There was a time when I made sauce in the service; Mom and Dad's basil joined the army! I was home on leave, due back to prepare the weekend meals at a small company mess hall. Armed with extra-virgin olive oil and fresh basil, I created a delicious sauce. That Sunday I watched the guys as they devoured my pasta in the "four-star mess hall," waiting for one, just one soldier, to pick up the ketchup. Thank God none did.

Every time a dried herb, such as thyme, parsley, or basil is added to a recipe, it should be ground between your fingers to release the natural oil and bouquet. Never ever shake a dried herb directly into a pot cooking on the stove; steam will enter the jar and cause the contents to deteriorate.

FREEZING

Keep a roll of masking tape, a marker, and waxed freezer paper placed conveniently near the freezer for wrapping and labeling fresh meat items. We all know how difficult it is to remove aluminum foil from frozen meats, so for optimum storage, rewrap supermarket meats in waxed freezer wrap.

Wrap meat in small portions of one or two servings. It is very easy to defrost more than one portion if needed, but very hard to break one frozen burger or chop from a mass of frozen meat. When buying chopped meat for the freezer, portion and preform it into patties before freezing.

Strong plastic freezer bags and/or aluminum foil are good for pastry items and vegetables. Take advantage of low seasonal prices on various vegetables and blanch and freeze them when they are in their prime. At mealtime, remove what is needed and mix with other vegetables for a garden assortment.

Keep *order* in your freezer! And keep it clean, thus avoiding any odors that are hard to get rid of. Keep an open plastic container filled with baking soda to eliminate freezer odors. Label everything wrapped with quantity and date, and be sure to use older items first. One of the most distressing things that can happen with your frozen food is freezer burn. It can be prevented if items are wrapped properly and rotated.

If your freezer can accommodate large quantities of food, it may be a good idea to use my inventory system. On large index cards, list each package with its contents, quantity, and date frozen. Keep each category, such as vegetables, meats, and pastries on separate cards. Mark each with a number that is listed on your index cards. This way, instead of doing the "freezer shuffle" when you need to browse, just look over your card or cards and plan from your easy chair; it saves time, labor, and money! Don't forget to cross off what you take out and to add on new items.

SUGGESTED CARD FILE SYSTEM

NO.	CATEGORY	ITEM	DATE
#06	Cooked Meals (leftovers)	1 Chicken Kiev	Aug. 16
#07	Vegetables	Approx. 2 cups buttered lima beans	Sept. 10
#08	Meat	1 large turkey leg with thigh meat	July 19

Now you will always be prepared to have a satisfying meal even when the clock is against you or you are not in the mood for cooking with love.

The following list gives suggested lengths of time for storing frozen foods, provided they were properly frozen and correctly wrapped and the freezer environment is at a constant 0° F. A thermometer for the freezer is a good investment.

MAXIMUM STORAGE TIME AT 0° F.
FOR FROZEN FOODS

Vegetables, plain	12 months
Vegetables, sauced	6 months
Fruits	12 months
Precooked frozen dinners	6–8 months
Bread and pizza	6 months
Most fish	6 months
Poultry	8 months
Meat, ground or organ	3–4 months
Meat, whole cuts	6–8 months

When planning your errands, do your grocery shopping last, and when in the supermarket, pick up your frozen items last. Inspect for signs of telltale defrosting, such as peas clumped together in plastic bags, boxes that are out of shape, ice cream oozing out of containers. Avoid buying frozen groceries that are sitting on the supermarket floor waiting to be placed in the freezer.

Keep all frozen items packed together, preferably in an insulated bag, if available. I always keep a large cooler in the trunk of my car for transporting the frozen foods during the trip home. The cooler also comes in handy when I bring food to friends, tasters, local television appearances, and for taking home some of Mom's goodies. As soon as you are home, put the frozen foods away immediately and remember to add them to your index system.

In winter, put groceries in the trunk, where it is cold; in summer, put them up front with you. If you leave your groceries behind at the store for delivery, take the frozen items with you.

Always, always keep in mind the outdoor temperature when you are driving your frozen and fresh foods home from the store. We have all had butter and ice cream melt in summer heat, but I once had the opposite experience in La-crosse, Wisconsin, where I was due to make a live appearance on the "Noon News." I drove from Minneapolis the night before the show, in good winter weather, -10° F. Without thinking, I left all the groceries in the trunk of the car.

The next morning I gathered my props and, after an hour in the heated studio, I reached for an egg. I banged it gently against the bowl to break the shell—nothing happened. I banged a little harder and still nothing, so I banged much harder. The bowl broke and peach cream poured over the table. The egg was frozen solid. I continued to walk through the recipe; luckily, I had the finished dish ready to show on camera.

Never defrost food that needs refrigeration outside of the refrigerator. Plan ahead to allow enough time for defrosting in the refrigerator or follow your microwave directions for defrosting. Most raw frozen foods, once defrosted, can be cooked and then refrozen later.

PLAN-AHEAD FREEZER MEALS

It's a good idea to keep cooked chicken parts in your freezer. I like chicken or turkey breast cutlets, three-quarters cooked, individually wrapped, that I can pop under the broiler or microwave with a topping of Parmesan cheese, zucchini, tarragon, lemon, or oil. Another good idea is pizza heros. Take French or Italian loaves of bread, slice in half lengthwise, and mound on sauce, seasonings, cheese, cooked ground meat, onions, or whatever. Wrap tightly and freeze. When you are looking for a snack or munchie, there it is.

With proper freezer use, you can cook one day and eat for four days. See "The Old Standbys" for good ideas on what to do with leftover turkey, a positive reason for buying a bigger bird than you need immediately.

Passing down recipes from generation to generation results in what I call good cooking; the rest of the world calls it gourmet cooking. The more we experiment and taste different foods, the more we want to discover new tastes and combinations.

It is never too late to learn to cook or too early to begin. The basis of learning goes back to getting in the kitchen at a very early age and being welcomed and feeling natural. My being in the kitchen when I was young with Mom and Dad, both great cooks, and their love of giving influenced my ideas and my work.

We enrolled six-year-old children in our Cooking with Love School and they were enthusiastic learners. So were some of our older students, especially one devoted couple in their early eighties who came to cooking late in life.

As I have told thousands of students, you can do it and, yes, you will do it, if you do it with love. We all have the ability to cook and cook well. Great chefs trust their ideas and are not afraid to improvise and show their creativity, something everyone has. Just like many things in life, if you say you can't, then you won't.

Today the so-called drudgery of preparing healthy and delicious meals is diminished by the increasing amount of kitchen aids at our disposal. But remember, with all of the gadgets, it's you, the preparer, who will influence the final outcome with your own creativity.

When you are planning a meal, quietly take a moment and visualize what each dish will look like. Think about the cake you are about to bake. Visualize the icing and how you will decorate it. You will be amazed at the perfect results you can achieve.

And, yes, as I've often said, if tonight you don't want to cook, *don't;* it probably won't taste good. This is a good time for one of your freezer meals or for dining *out!*

II.
Cooking for Two with Love

RECIPES FOR TWO

Shrimps à la Provençal
Bananas d'Amore

All-Purpose Vinaigrette Salad Dressing
Veal Madeline
Leeks Parmesan

Princess Soup
Caraway Carrots
Chicken with Brandy Sauce
Fruit Compote

❖

THREE QUICK RECIPES

Pasta with Broccoli
Fresh Fish Fillets à la Anthony
Veal Casino

❖

THREE COOK-AND-FREEZE RECIPES

Beef and Onions in Beer
Oven Beef Stew
Chicken Rice Pilaf

❖

Dinner for two. It can mean a woman inviting a man or a man inviting a woman over for a knock-'em-dead meal designed to dazzle and delight and impress, or maybe seduce. It can be an invitation to high romance, the start of something big. Dinner for two can also mean a working husband and a working wife walking in the front door after a long day on the job, both needing to relax, unwind, spend time together. When you are cooking with love, the same principles apply, whether you're looking across the table at the new love in your life or at the partner with whom you have shared ten years of dinners—and breakfasts. Select good, fresh food, cook it properly, serve it graciously, and celebrate.

A lot of twosomes think it's easier to eat out. Maybe it is a bit easier, but it's a lot more expensive, less creative, and not nearly as much fun. There is no kitchen like your own kitchen and no better way to control the quality of your meals and the mood around you than by doing it yourself. Every now and then it's nice to send out for a pepperoni pizza or some Szechuan specialties, but never underestimate your ability to prepare meals as tasty and appealing as anything you can order in most neighborhood restaurants.

The suggestions that follow aren't written in stone. The

meat prepared with a tangy white wine sauce in Veal Madeline can just as successfully be chicken or even a minute steak—any kind of poultry or meat that is thin enough to cook properly by sautéing and will be complemented by the sauce.

The following three menus have all the ingredients for a splendidly successful dinner for two. They are simple to prepare and don't take long. They call for fresh, wholesome ingredients to be prepared with that little bit of a twist that makes for flair. Each menu demonstrates a quality vital to cooking with love—balance and variety in taste, color, and texture.

Good bread is an important part of a well-rounded meal and is a major source of carbohydrates. Bread seems to go out the window when the word *diet* comes up. But if you put a good-quality baked bread or a home-baked loaf on the table, everyone reaches for some. I like crusty, chewy Italian and French bread. If you are watching your cholesterol, pour a little plate of extra-virgin olive oil for dipping the bread instead of using butter. And by all means dip your bread into these one-dish pots and mop up the good sauce.

❖ *MENU FOR TWO* ❖

SHRIMPS À LA PROVENÇAL   STEAMED BROCCOLI SPEARS

WHITE RICE   BANANAS D'AMORE

Luscious, perfectly cooked (not overcooked) shrimp in a tomato-based sauce are delightfully complemented with plain white rice and bright green, delicately steamed (again, not overcooked) broccoli.

Start the rice first, following the directions on the box. The rice will take about 20 minutes, the broccoli about 10 to 12 minutes, leaving you time to prepare the shrimp.

If you have a chafing dish or an electric buffet pan, Bananas d'Amore is a dramatic dish to prepare at the table. Light the tablespoon of rum with a match and dazzle your guest. This easy dessert can also be made at the kitchen stove.

SHRIMPS À LA PROVENÇAL

3/4 pound medium shrimp
2 tablespoons unsalted butter
2 tablespoons vegetable oil
2 cloves garlic, peeled
6 plum tomatoes (very ripe fresh or canned),
    coarsely chopped
2 bay leaves
1/2 teaspoon lemon juice
1/8 teaspoon dried thyme
1 tablespoon chopped fresh parsley
Freshly ground pepper to taste
Salt, if desired

Shell and devein the shrimp.

Combine the butter and oil in a skillet over medium heat. Add the garlic and sauté until brown. Remove and discard the garlic. To the skillet, add the chopped tomatoes and bay leaves and cook about 5 minutes.

Add the shrimp, lemon juice, herbs, and seasonings. Stir and cook until shrimp are pink, about 5 minutes. Do not overcook. Serve immediately.

BANANAS D'AMORE

2 ripe bananas
3 tablespoons unsalted butter
6 tablespoons unsweetened cocoa
5 tablespoons brown sugar
Dash of vanilla
1/4 cup plus 1 tablespoon dark rum
Vanilla ice cream

Peel the bananas and slice them in half both lengthwise and crosswise.

Melt the butter in a chafing dish, electric buffet pan, or skillet over low heat. Sauté the bananas lightly on both sides, keeping them firm; remove them to a platter.

Remove the pan from the heat and add the cocoa, stirring with a wooden spoon. Slowly add the sugar, vanilla, and 1/4 cup rum, stirring constantly. Return to low heat, taking care that the mixture does not burn. Add the bananas and roll them gently in the chocolate mixture. Remove from the heat, add the remaining tablespoon rum, and flame. Serve on individual dessert plates with vanilla ice cream.

❖ *MENU FOR TWO* ❖

TOSSED GREENS IN ALL-PURPOSE	LEEKS PARMESAN
VINAIGRETTE SALAD DRESSING	VANILLA ICE CREAM WITH
VEAL MADELINE	AMARETTO

No bottled salad dressing can ever match the tangy flavor of home-prepared vinaigrette dressing, and nothing could be easier to make. Some people claim oil-and-vinegar dressings must be made on the spot, fresh for each new salad. I am all in favor of making cooking easy on yourself and I see nothing wrong with preparing a dressing beforehand. Look for a variety of greens—chicory, Boston lettuce, watercress—to make an attractive salad.

Veal Madeline is an elegant, easy, and astonishingly quick dish to cook. If the cutlets you bought are not very thin, place them between sheets of wax paper on a hard surface and pound them with a mallet or rolling pin. The cutlets should be about ¼ inch thick.

A splash of Amaretto liqueur—or use Cassis if you like the dark berry flavor—makes everyday vanilla ice cream something special. Several of my dessert recipes call for liqueurs. In many liquor stores you can buy these in tiny bottles. Get a variety and find out which flavors you like, without making a big investment.

All-PURPOSE VINAIGRETTE SALAD DRESSING

³/₄ cup extra-virgin olive oil
¹/₄ cup white-wine vinegar
2 tablespoons Dijon mustard
1 teaspoon salt
¹/₈ teaspoon freshly ground pepper
1 medium clove garlic, crushed
¹/₂ teaspoon sugar
1 tablespoon water

Blend all ingredients thoroughly, either in a blender or by shaking in a jar. Save in a covered jar in the refrigerator. When needed, shake and pour over salad greens of your choice or use in recipes that call for a vinaigrette. *Makes about 1¹/₄ cups.*

VEAL MADELINE

4 tablespoons unsalted butter or margarine
2 thin veal cutlets
2 tablespoons finely chopped scallions
1/4 cup dry white wine
1 teaspoon Worcestershire sauce
Dash of bitters
Freshly ground pepper to taste
Chopped fresh parsley for garnish

In a large skillet, heat 2 tablespoons butter or margarine until hot and foamy but not brown. Add the veal and sauté quickly over high heat on both sides to desired doneness, about 3 minutes per side. Remove to a heated platter.

Lower the heat; add the scallions and wine and stir well, scraping the bottom of the skillet to loosen drippings. Add the Worcestershire, bitters, pepper, and remaining butter or margarine. Heat, stirring constantly, until the butter melts. Pour sauce over the veal and sprinkle with parsley.

LEEKS PARMESAN

4 medium-to-large leeks
1 tablespoon unsalted butter
1 tablespoon olive oil
1 clove garlic, crushed
$1/4$ teaspoon dried savory
Freshly ground pepper to taste
Salt, if desired
2 tablespoons grated Parmesan cheese

Cut off the root from the leeks and most of the green leaves so that you keep about 2 inches of green and the white part. Cut in half lengthwise and wash in several changes of water to remove all sand. Pat dry.

Melt the butter with the oil in a skillet and add the garlic. Discard the garlic when brown. Add the leeks and savory, and sauté until soft, about 8 minutes. Season with pepper, add salt if desired. Turn off the heat, and sprinkle with the Parmesan. Cover and let sit for a minute, then serve.

❖ *MENU FOR TWO* ❖

PRINCESS SOUP   CHICKEN WITH BRANDY SAUCE
CARAWAY CARROTS   FRUIT COMPOTE

I often sing the praises of a good chicken stock because of all the wonderful things you can use it for. (See page 102 for my Basic Chicken Stock recipe.) One of my favorites is Princess Soup, a light soup with a touch of egg and cheese, a fine beginning for many meals. You can make this dish with a good-quality canned stock or broth, but it won't be as terrific as with homemade stock.

Carrots and caraway seeds are a natural combination. Try it, even if you think you don't like carrots.

PRINCESS SOUP

1 egg
1/8 teaspoon freshly ground nutmeg
2 cups chicken stock (see Basic Chicken Stock, p. 102)
Freshly ground pepper to taste
1 tablespoon grated Parmesan cheese

Break the egg into a small bowl, add the nutmeg, and beat well with a wire whisk. Bring the chicken stock to a boil and pour in the egg, stirring constantly with the whisk. The egg will float in small pieces.

Pour the soup into individual serving bowls, add a twist of ground pepper, sprinkle with Parmesan, and serve.

CARAWAY CARROTS

1 tablespoon unsalted butter.
2 tablespoons water
1 small onion, thinly sliced
2 large or 3 medium carrots, cut into matchstick strips
$1/4$ teaspoon caraway seeds
$1/8$ teaspoon ground coriander
$1/8$ teaspoon white pepper

Heat the butter and water in a small skillet. Add the onion and sauté until the onion is soft. Add the carrots and seasonings. Cook, covered, over medium heat, stirring or shaking occasionally, until carrots are cooked but still crunchy.

CHICKEN WITH BRANDY SAUCE

1 tablespoon unsalted butter
1 medium-to-large chicken breast, cut in half
2 shallots, or 1 small onion, minced
4 tablespoons brandy
$^1/_2$ cup milk
$^1/_2$ cup heavy cream
1 teaspoon cornstarch dissolved in 2 tablespoons
   water
1 teaspoon dried marjoram
Freshly ground pepper to taste
Salt, if desired
Fresh parsley sprigs for garnish
Optional:
$^3/_4$ pound fresh mushrooms, chopped
2 tablespoons butter

Over medium heat, melt the butter in a large skillet. Add the chicken, skin side down; cover and cook until brown, about 12 minutes. Turn the chicken over and continue cooking, uncovered, until done, about 10 to 15 minutes. Remove to a warm serving platter. Defat juices if necessary.

Add the shallots or onion and the brandy to the skillet and stir, scraping the drippings from the bottom of the pan with a wooden spoon. Cook over high heat to reduce contents slightly.

When the shallots or onion are tender, lower the heat and briskly stir in the milk, cream, cornstarch mixture, marjoram, pepper, and salt if desired. (A whisk is better than a wooden spoon for this.) When sauce starts to boil and becomes bubbly, simmer approximately 4 minutes longer. Spoon sauce over chicken breasts, and garnish with fresh parsley.

If desired, sauté fresh mushrooms in butter, and add the mushrooms to the finished brandy sauce before serving.

FRUIT COMPOTE

1 navel orange
1 small banana
1 cup pineapple chunks, canned or fresh
1 teaspoon cinnamon sugar
2 ounces fruity liqueur (e.g., raspberry or orange
    liqueur; cherry, peach, or blueberry schnapps)

Peel the orange and cut into chunks. Be sure to remove white veins. Peel and slice the banana. Combine orange, banana, and pineapple in a bowl and toss with cinnamon sugar. Arrange in individual dessert bowls. Before serving, splash with liqueur.

THREE QUICK RECIPES

At the end of the day, working couples have too little time in the kitchen. Here are three easy recipes to get you through tired times with ease.

Pasta is a great rush-hour savior, a kitchen staple with myriad possibilities. Pasta doesn't have to mean spaghetti with a bottled tomato sauce over it. Experiment with the different varieties. You can adapt the following recipe for ziti or regati, bow-tie pasta or delicate cappellini. Instead of broccoli, try fresh asparagus cut into $1/2$-inch pieces, green beans, or spinach. Pasta is also wonderful with leftover diced cooked chicken, turkey, or ham. See "The Old Standbys" (pages 43–74) for more pasta suggestions and recipes.

PASTA WITH BROCCOLI

$1/2$ bunch broccoli
$1/4$ cup olive oil
1 medium red bell pepper, sliced into thin strips
1 clove garlic, peeled
$1/4$ cup water
$1/4$ cup dry white wine
8 ounces pasta, such as fettuccine or linguine
2 tablespoons unsalted butter
$1/2$ cup grated Parmesan cheese
Freshly ground pepper to taste
Salt, if desired

Wash the broccoli. Trim off the leaves and tough ends of each stalk and peel the skin with a vegetable peeler. Cut the stalk into $1/2$ -inch pieces and the head into small florets.

Heat the olive oil over moderate heat in a large skillet. Add the broccoli, red pepper strips, and garlic; cook 1 minute, stirring frequently. Discard the garlic when brown. Add the water and wine. Cover and cook over low heat until the broccoli is just tender but firm, about 5 minutes.

Cook the pasta in a large saucepan as directed on pages 54–55. Drain, return to saucepan and toss with butter. Stir in the broccoli mixture, cheese, and pepper, and salt if desired.

FRESH FISH FILLETS À LA ANTHONY

Suggestion: Serve with leftover cooked rice that you have stored in a thick plastic bag ready to be reheated.

4 tablespoons unsalted butter
Juice of ½ lemon
2 tablespoons chopped Italian parsley
1 tablespoon capers
1 cup dry white wine
Liberal amount of white pepper
Salt, if desired
2 large fillets of your favorite lean fish (4 ounces each)
Watercress for garnish
Lemon slices for garnish

Place all the ingredients except the fish and garnishes in a skillet and cook over low heat for a few minutes. Add the fish, cover, and continue cooking until the fish appears flaky, about 5 minutes. *Do not overcook!* Remove the fish to a warm serving platter. Reduce the sauce to about half, and pour over the fish. Garnish with circle of watercress and lemon slices. Serve immediately.

VEAL CASINO

This recipe won me raves when I cooked it for my first appearance at Trump Plaza Hotel & Casino.

2 veal steaks or chops
Flour for dusting
3 tablespoons olive oil
2 tablespoons unsalted butter
4 plum tomatoes, chopped
1 large or 2 small artichoke hearts, sliced
4 green olives, chopped
2 scallions, chopped
Dash of bitters
$^1/_4$ teaspoon dry mustard
Freshly ground pepper to taste

Lightly dust the chops with flour. In a large skillet, melt the oil and butter. Sauté the chops on each side for approximately 4 minutes per side, depending on thickness. Remove to a heated platter and keep warm.

Add all other ingredients to the skillet and cook approximately 6 to 8 minutes. Spoon sauce over chops and serve.

THREE COOK-AND-FREEZE RECIPES

I like the following cook-ahead recipes for a working couple because you get two meals and do the work for just one. Beef stews and pilaf freeze well and, what's more, they taste just as good the second time around. Each of the following recipes makes enough for two dinners for two.

BEEF AND ONIONS IN BEER

2 pounds beef, such as chuck steak, cut into short, thin slices, fat removed
4 tablespoons flour
2 tablespoons olive oil
1 pound onions, thinly sliced
2 tablespoons unsalted butter
2 tablespoons distilled white vinegar
$1/2$ teaspoon dried thyme
1 cup beef stock
12 ounces dark beer
2 bay leaves
Freshly ground pepper to taste
1 teaspoon dark brown sugar

Preheat oven to 325°F.

Sprinkle the sliced beef with 2 tablespoons flour, making sure all the pieces are completely coated. Heat the oil in a large flameproof casserole, add the beef and onion slices, and brown quickly. With a slotted spoon, remove the beef and onions and set aside.

Heat the butter in the same casserole and add the remaining 2 tablespoons flour, stirring until the flour and butter are combined and starting to brown. Still stirring, add the vinegar, thyme, beef stock, and beer. Continue stirring until the sauce is smooth and evenly thickened. Return the meat and onions to the casserole and add the bay leaves and pepper. Sprinkle the brown sugar over the top. Cover and cook in the oven for 2 hours.

Serve half the recipe and freeze the rest for another evening.

OVEN BEEF STEW

2 pounds beef stew meat, cut into 1-inch cubes
1 tablespoon olive oil
Salt, if desired
Freshly ground pepper to taste
1 clove garlic, minced
5 small onions (2 chopped, 2 sliced, 1 whole)
3/4 teaspoon dried thyme
1 bay leaf
2/3 cup chopped fresh parsley
3 cups beef stock
4 whole cloves
6 carrots, peeled and cut into 2-inch pieces
4 medium potatoes, cut into 2-inch pieces (unpeeled)
About 1 pound rutabaga or turnips, peeled and cut
    into 2-inch pieces (2 cups)
1/2 pound fresh mushrooms, cut in half
2 tablespoons flour
1/4 cup cold water

Preheat oven to 500°F.

Place the beef chunks and oil in a Dutch oven or heavy flameproof covered casserole. Sprinkle with salt, if desired, and pepper; add the garlic and 2 of the onions, which you have finely chopped, and mix. Brown, uncovered, in oven for 20 minutes.

Add the thyme, bay leaf, 1/3 cup parsley, and the beef stock; lower the oven temperature to 350°F., cover, and cook 40 minutes.

Slice 2 of the remaining onions and stick the cloves into

the remaining whole onion. Add the onions to the stew with the carrots, potatoes, and rutabaga. Cook, covered, for another 45 minutes. Add the mushrooms and cook 10 minutes longer.

Remove the stew from the oven. Mix the flour with the cold water, and stir into the stew. Simmer 5 to 8 minutes on top of the stove, until the gravy thickens slightly. Sprinkle with the remaining $^1/_3$ cup chopped parsley before serving. Freeze half the stew for another evening.

CHICKEN RICE PILAF

$^2/_3$ cup uncooked long-grain rice
$^2/_3$ cup thin spaghetti broken into 2-inch pieces
$^1/_3$ cup olive oil
3 cups chicken stock
1 cup fresh or thawed frozen broccoli florets
$^1/_4$ teaspoon dried thyme, crushed
1 cup cooked chicken, cut in julienne strips
$^1/_2$ cup sliced scallions
$^1/_4$ cup chopped walnuts
$^1/_4$ cup diced red bell pepper

In a saucepan, sauté the rice and spaghetti in olive oil until golden, stirring often. Add the chicken stock and bring to a boil.

Add the broccoli and thyme. Cover and simmer 15 minutes, or until rice is tender, stirring occasionally. Add the remaining ingredients and heat through.

Serve half the recipe and freeze the rest for another meal.

One last thought: If you are planning an intimate dinner for two and you're a little nervous about pulling things off without a hitch, do absolutely *everything* that can be done the evening before; and when your meal is over, leave for the next day absolutely *everything* that can be left until tomorrow. For example, on the night before:

- Wash salad greens; pat dry with paper towels and store the greens in a plastic bag in your refrigerator.

- Make the salad dressing.

- Make the dessert or any other part of the meal that can be prepared ahead. If your recipe calls for chopped onions, do the chopping ahead of time and store the onions in the freezer.

- Organize the cooking ingredients you will be using. Think through the recipe directions, step by step, in your mind and line up on the counter your box of rice, bag of flour, spices, et cetera, as well as bowls, measuring spoons, and cups.

- Set a delectable table with plates, flatware, napkins, and wineglasses.

- Have coffee cups, spoons, and after-dinner items like cookies, dessert, or liqueurs organized separately and ready to go.

After dinner:

- Don't spoil a lovely mood by fussing with a

messy table; put the dirty dishes in the refrigerator and wash them the next day.

Think the meal through ahead of time, anticipate what
you will need, and be prepared. Now you can relax and enjoy
the meal.

III.

The Old Standbys

CHICKEN AND TURKEY

Stir-Fried Chicken Breasts with Snow Peas
Chicken with Fennel
Bourbon Chicken
Chicken in Wine-and-Caper Sauce
Turkey or Chicken Divan
Curried Turkey or Chicken
Turkey Hash

❖

PASTA

Spaghetti and Tuna
Rigatoni with Brussels Sprouts
Pasta with Marinara Sauce
Pasta with Pesto
Pesto Cream Sauce
Fettuccine with Peas in Cheese Sauce
Pasta alla Puttanesca
Ground Veal with Spinach Noodles

❖

EGGS

Vegetable-Cheese Frittata
French Mushroom Omelette
Egg Foo Yung
Old-Country Quiche

❖

GROUND MEAT

Veal and Lima Bean Casserole
Grandma's Meat Loaf
Mom's Meatballs
Shepherd's Pie
Skillet Lamb

❖

Everyone who plans meals will prepare over and over again, in some new or old recipe, chicken, pasta, ground meat, and eggs. Each of these old standbys can be made in the most simple way or can be translated into elegant dining.

CHICKEN AND TURKEY

Chicken is one of the most popular items in our kitchen repertoire. It is easy to cook, allows great variety in menu planning, and is recommended for today's light eating. Today, all turkeys and chickens are processed and brought to the marketplace in a short time. Few of us see chickens and turkeys in their undressed state with their feathers, except for farm families and hunters. The days of going to the poultry market, where you would choose your live chicken, duck, or turkey before it was tagged and taken off to be slaughtered, are over, although you can still see feathered birds at the open-air markets in Paris.

When you buy an all-purpose whole broiler/fryer, allow about ³/₄ pound of bone-in chicken per serving; with boneless cuts, approximate ¹/₄ pound per serving. Because I appear on television shows and at food fairs all over the country, I know different supermarkets sell different sizes of chicken breasts. Usually a medium-to-large breast (bone in) of about 20 to 24 ounces will serve two people. Cutlets are boneless, skinless breasts prepared by a butcher.

Turkey is as nutritious and economical as chicken and is now widely available fresh in smaller sizes, as well as in parts and boneless cuts. I love to cook a large turkey because you can use the cooked meat in many recipes.

When you buy a 16-to-20-pound frozen turkey, it will take up to three days to thaw in the refrigerator. Do not thaw any meat, poultry, or fish on the kitchen counter; always place it on a plate in the refrigerator.

Refrigerate all poultry before and after cooking and serving. I always use a meat thermometer to cook a turkey. Cook an unstuffed bird to 180°F. to 185°F., with the thermometer placed through a thigh (not touching bone). A stuffed bird should read 165°F. with the thermometer placed through the carcass into the center of the stuffing.

Pack the stuffing loosely in the turkey; it will expand during the cooking. Do not allow a cooked turkey to sit around for excessive periods of time. Remove the leftover stuffing immediately after the meal and refrigerate the turkey and the stuffing separately. After you have carved it all and have frozen the meat for other meals, the carcass will make a great turkey soup (page 104). The easy recipes that follow can use chicken or turkey interchangeably.

STIR-FRIED CHICKEN BREASTS WITH SNOW PEAS

This is quick and colorful. Serve with rice.

2 medium-to-large chicken breasts (4 halves), skinned
  and boned
2 tablespoons cornstarch
3 tablespoons water
1 teaspoon sugar
2 tablespoons soy sauce
3 tablespoons peanut oil
1 cup sliced scallions
$^{1}/_{2}$ pound snow peas
1 cup sliced mushrooms
1 cup whole fresh or thawed frozen corn kernels
$^{1}/_{2}$ cup chicken stock
Freshly ground pepper to taste

Wash the chicken and pat it dry. Slice the breasts into strips. In a small jar, shake together the cornstarch, water, sugar, and soy sauce.

Heat the oil in a large skillet. When it is hot, stir-fry the scallions for a few minutes. Add the chicken and cook another 1 to 2 minutes, stirring constantly. Add the snow peas, mushrooms, corn, and chicken stock. Stir rapidly to mix and heat through. Pour in the cornstarch mixture and cook another 2 to 3 minutes. Serve immediately with freshly ground pepper. *Serves 4.*

CHICKEN WITH FENNEL

An easy, healthy dish that uses no oil or butter in cooking.

2 medium-to-large chicken breasts, cut in half and
     boned
1 medium onion, minced
2 cloves garlic
Juice of 1/2 lemon
1 teaspoon fennel seeds

Place the chicken breast halves in a large skillet, skin side down, and brown them quickly. Reduce the heat and add the onion and garlic. Cover and cook about 15 to 20 minutes.

Remove the chicken from the pan and defat the juices. Return the chicken and juices that have accumulated to the pan, and add the lemon juice and fennel seeds. Cover and cook until the chicken is done, approximately 15 minutes. *Serves 4.*

BOURBON CHICKEN

Asked by my TV producer to cook something appropriate for our live broadcast from Churchill Downs, I created a great Derby sit-down dinner with all-American chicken and Kentucky bourbon.

2 tablespoons unsalted butter
2 medium-to-large chicken breasts, cut in half and
   boned
1/2 cup bourbon
4 to 6 shallots, sliced
1/2 cup heavy cream
1/8 teaspoon nutmeg
1/4 teaspoon white pepper

Melt the butter in a large pan. Place the chicken breasts, skin side down, in the pan in which you have heated the butter, and quickly brown over high heat. Sprinkle 1/4 cup bourbon over the chicken and ignite it. Add the shallots and cook until the flames go out, then add the remaining bourbon. Cover the pan and cook over low heat for approximately 12 to 14 minutes, until the chicken is done. Transfer the chicken to a serving platter and keep warm.

Defat the pan juices, if needed, then add the cream, nutmeg, and pepper. Simmer just until the sauce thickens. Pour the sauce over the chicken and serve. *Serves 4.*

CHICKEN IN WINE-AND-CAPER SAUCE

8 small chicken cutlets, or 4 large turkey cutlets
$1/4$ cup olive oil
1 small onion, minced
$1/2$ cup dry white wine
$1/4$ teaspoon dried sage
Juice of $1/2$ lemon
1 tablespoon capers
1 tablespoon chopped fresh parsley

Pound the chicken cutlets between wax paper to about $1/8$- to $1/4$-inch thickness. Sauté the cutlets in the oil, about $2^{1}/2$ minutes per side. When they are cooked, remove to a warm platter. Add the onion, wine, and sage to the pan and reduce to three-quarters of the volume.

Turn off the heat. Stir in the lemon juice, parsley, and capers. Return the chicken to the sauce and heat through. Serve immediately. *Serves 4.*

TURKEY OR CHICKEN DIVAN

2 tablespoons unsalted butter
2 tablespoons flour
1 cup turkey or chicken stock
$\frac{1}{2}$ cup milk
$\frac{1}{4}$ cup dry white wine or dry sherry
Freshly ground pepper to taste
Salt, if desired
Liberal grating of fresh nutmeg
1 cup heavy cream
$\frac{1}{4}$ cup grated Parmesan cheese
Two 10-ounce packages frozen broccoli or asparagus
    spears, or 1 large head fresh broccoli or 1 large
    bunch fresh asparagus, cooked until just done
10 to 12 slices cooked turkey meat or chicken
Paprika

Preheat the oven to 375°F.

Heat the butter and blend in the flour over low heat to make a roux, stirring constantly until lightly browned. Slowly stir in the stock and milk; add the wine or sherry, pepper, salt if desired, and nutmeg, and continue cooking until the volume is reduced by half. Add the cream and grated Parmesan and let the mixture thicken.

Butter a flameproof casserole. Lay the cooked broccoli or asparagus on the bottom of the casserole and add the turkey or chicken slices. Pour the sumptuous sauce generously over the top of the meat slices, and sprinkle with paprika. Place the casserole in the oven for 20 minutes, then under the broiler to brown for 1 or 2 minutes. *Serves 6.*

CURRIED TURKEY OR CHICKEN

Serve over rice, with two or more of the suggested relishes offered in separate bowls to the side.

2 tablespoons unsalted butter
2 tablespoons flour
2 1/2 teaspoons curry powder
1 tablespoon lemon juice
1 cup chicken stock
1 cup heavy cream
1 to 1 1/2 pounds cooked turkey or chicken,
  cut in pieces

RELISHES:
  1 cup raisins
  1 cup coarsely chopped peanuts
  1 cup chopped green bell pepper
  1/2 to 1 cup toasted coconut
  1 cup chutney

Heat the butter and blend in the flour over low heat to make a roux. Stir in the curry powder. Gradually blend in the lemon juice and stock, stirring continually. Continue cooking until the volume is reduced by half. Add the cream and let the mixture thicken.

Add the turkey or chicken meat and let simmer, without boiling, for approximately 15 minutes. *Serves 4.*

TURKEY HASH

To be enjoyed at breakfast, brunch, or while watching a late TV movie.

1 cup turkey gravy
$1/2$ cup minced onion
1 cup boiled potatoes, unpeeled and diced
$1/2$ cup thinly sliced celery
$1/2$ cup sliced mushrooms
3 healthy pinches of parsley flakes
Fresh grating of nutmeg
2 pinches of ground rosemary
2 cups diced cooked turkey

Heat the gravy in a broiler-proof pan and add the onion, potatoes, celery, and mushrooms. Bring to a boil, reduce the heat, and simmer about 8 minutes.

Add the parsley flakes, nutmeg, and rosemary. Add the turkey and blend thoroughly. Cook another 5 minutes. Put the pan under the broiler for a few minutes until hash is crisp on top. *Serves 4.*

PASTA

Pasta delivers a bona fide nutritional boost. The variety and shapes are as imaginative as the foods and sauces that accompany them. Delicate shapes such as angel's hair and spaghettini necessitate a light dressing; larger shapes like rigatoni and rote can be paired with vegetables and heavier sauces. There are so many varieties that you could make a different pasta recipe every day of the year.

Today we see pasta on menus in many forms: as cold salads, as an appetizer with seafood, and as a main course. We have come a long way from the days when pasta meant spaghetti swimming in red sauce.

It is no wonder that pasta is a favorite food of most children. In my cooking school, six-year-old little chefs proudly built towers of lasagna to take home to share with their moms, dads, brothers, and sisters.

Do not cook pasta past the stage of firmness—al dente, as the Italians say—and you will enjoy it more. Remember when measuring before cooking that 2 ounces per person is perfect for an appetizer portion, and 3 to 4 ounces for a main course. As you know, pasta grows as it cooks to nearly double its original size. Fresh egg noodles do not expand as much.

The proper cooking of pasta is very important. I start with 6 quarts of fresh cold water in a large covered saucepan for

54

every pound of pasta. I usually search my refrigerator, looking for bits and pieces of vegetables left over from other recipes, like a broccoli stalk or a small piece of cauliflower that will otherwise wind up in the garbage. I add these vegetable bits to the water before boiling for flavor and whatever additional nutrients they impart to the pasta. Remove the vegetables before adding the pasta.

At this point, *most* of my colleagues would add about 2 tablespoons salt to the boiling water. I do *not*. *I do not add any salt.* Try it both ways; you be the judge. Instead, I add 1 tablespoon olive oil just before adding the pasta. It prevents the pasta from sticking together and adds a little extra flavor. When this is done, I add the pasta gradually to keep the water temperature from dropping too low. I place the cover on the pan and within a minute or so the water returns to a ferocious boiling state. I then remove the cover. I know most packaged dried pasta comes with directions on the bag or box, but forget those directions. You know I don't want you to labor over many things, but pasta needs attention and an occasional stirring. I like to use a pasta fork, a great tool for stirring and serving pasta.

Because fresh pasta is made with egg, it usually floats to the top in a matter of minutes; it is then ready. Dried boxed or bagged pasta usually necessitates several more minutes, but there are no real guidelines. *You* must taste it during the cooking process to judge if it is al dente, meaning a little chewy to the tooth, which is the preferable texture for maximum enjoyment. Since I do not rinse the pasta after it is drained (immediately after cooking), you must be ready to sauce it and serve it. Pasta my way waits for no man; man waits for *it*.

Here are some quick and easy recipes. Be creative and combine pasta with diced ham, turkey, chicken, and vegetable leftovers.

SPAGHETTI AND TUNA

9$\frac{1}{4}$ ounces canned tuna fish packed in vegetable oil
2 tablespoons olive oil
2 tablespoons unsalted butter
1 clove garlic
One 28-ounce can Italian plum tomatoes, drained and
    coarsely chopped
Freshly ground pepper to taste
12 ounces spaghetti or linguine
Sprigs of Italian parsley for garnish

Drain the oil from the canned tuna fish. In a skillet, heat
the olive oil and butter, and sauté the garlic and tomatoes
for 20 minutes. Remove garlic when brown. Add the tuna
fish to the sauce, and break it apart with a fork. Cook over
low heat for 10 minutes more; add pepper to taste.

Cook the spaghetti or linguine al dente. Serve the sauce
over the pasta and garnish with parsley sprigs. *Serves 4.*

RIGATONI WITH BRUSSELS SPROUTS

4 tablespoons olive oil
2 tablespoons unsalted butter or margarine
1 medium onion, diced
1 cup diced ham steak
1 1/2 cups Brussels sprouts, cut in half
1/2 teaspoon dried basil
1/4 teaspoon dried thyme
Freshly ground pepper to taste
12 ounces rigatoni
Grated Parmesan cheese
Optional:
4 tablespoons sour cream

Heat the oil and butter or margarine in a large pan and sauté the onion and ham until the onion is soft. Add the Brussels sprouts. Season with the basil, thyme, and pepper.

Meanwhile, cook the rigatoni al dente, and add 2 tablespoons or more of the pasta water to the sauce. Cook, covered, until the Brussels sprouts are done, about 14 minutes.

Serve the pasta with the sauce and grated Parmesan cheese. If you wish, you can mix 1 tablespoon sour cream per person into the sauce at serving time. *Serves 4.*

PASTA WITH MARINARA SAUCE

You can double this recipe and freeze the leftovers for another time. If you wish to add meat, sauté chopped meat, meatballs, or sausages briefly in a little oil. Drain off the fat and add the meat to the sauce for the second part of its cooking.
Serve with your favorite pasta.

1 small onion, chopped
2 cloves garlic
4 tablespoons olive oil
1 large can (2 pounds 3 ounces) Italian tomatoes, with juice
1 teaspoon salt
2 pinches of dried basil
1 pinch of dried thyme
Freshly ground pepper to taste
1 pound pasta of your choice
Optional:
3 ounces tomato paste
3 ounces water

In a large pan, sauté the onion and garlic in the oil for about 5 minutes. Chop the tomatoes coarsely, and add with the juices to the onion. Add the salt, basil, thyme, and pepper. Cook, covered, 10 minutes; stir and cook, uncovered, for an additional 20 to 25 minutes.

If you wish to thicken the sauce, add 3 ounces of tomato paste and an equal amount of water at the start of cooking.
Serves 4.

PASTA WITH PESTO

You can make this wonderful summer sauce easily in a food processor. Borrow one if need be. Pesto freezes easily for many enjoyable meals year-round.

A teaspoon of pesto adds zest to cold gazpacho or similar soups. Add 1 tablespoon to each cup of ricotta cheese stuffing for filled pastas or lasagna, or 1 tablespoon per cup of sour cream for a cocktail-party dip. Thin out a little pesto with additional olive oil and use on baked, broiled, or grilled meat, chicken, or fish.

1 1/2 to 2 cups loosely packed basil leaves
1/4 cup Italian parsley leaves
2 tablespoons walnut pieces
1 tablespoon pine nuts (pignoli)
1 clove garlic, or more to taste
3 tablespoons unsalted butter
1/4 teaspoon white pepper
Pinch of freshly ground nutmeg
1/4 teaspoon orange peel
1/2 cup grated Parmesan cheese, or 4 ounces, cut up
3 ounces olive oil, or more if needed
1 pound spaghetti or linguine

Wash and dry the basil and parsley leaves. Blanch the walnuts and pine nuts.

Place the knife blade in the food processor. Add the walnuts, pine nuts, garlic, butter, pepper, nutmeg, and orange peel. With the machine running, add the cheese down the

59

feed tube. Add the greens down the tube and process until you have a thick paste.

While the machine is still running, slowly and steadily trickle the olive oil down the tube, and continue processing until the paste is smooth. *Makes about 1 1/2 cups.*

Serve with hot pasta of your choice. Dilute the pesto with 1 tablespoon pasta water per portion and toss with the hot pasta. Additional pasta water can be added if a thinner consistency is desired. About 1 tablespoon pesto to 2 ounces of pasta is average for a serving, since this is a concentrated sauce.

PESTO CREAM SAUCE

This sauce is delicious and easy! Just mix and heat 4 tablespoons of the pesto with 1/2 cup heavy cream for four 2-ounce servings of pasta, or as a sauce over manicotti or ravioli.

FETTUCCINE WITH PEAS
IN CHEESE SAUCE

$^{1}/_{2}$ cup unsalted butter
$^{1}/_{2}$ cup fresh or thawed frozen peas
$^{1}/_{2}$ cup sliced mushrooms
$^{1}/_{2}$ cup light cream
$^{1}/_{2}$ cup grated Parmesan cheese
Freshly ground pepper to taste
Salt, if desired
1 pound fresh or dried fettuccine

Melt the butter over low heat. Add the peas and mushrooms and cook over low heat about 3 minutes.

Add the cream to the sauce, stirring constantly, until the sauce thickens, about 5 minutes. Add the grated Parmesan, pepper, and salt if desired, and cook another 2 to 3 minutes.

Meanwhile, cook the pasta al dente, and toss with sauce. *Serves 4.*

PASTA ALLA PUTTANESCA

This dish is said to have originated with the streetwalkers in ancient Naples, when they needed a quick hot meal. That is why it is called puttanesca. *This spicy and tasty sauce is one of my favorites.*

2 cloves garlic
4 tablespoons olive oil
2 anchovy fillets
One 35-ounce can Italian plum tomatoes, undrained
    and coarsely chopped
1 dozen black olives, chopped
1 small pimento, chopped
2 sprigs basil
1 tablespoon capers
1/4 teaspoon dried hot red pepper flakes
Freshly ground pepper to taste
1 tablespoon finely chopped fresh parsley
1 pound linguine

Sauté the garlic in the oil, and add the anchovies. As soon as the anchovies start to dissolve in the oil, add the tomatoes with their juice, the olives, pimento, basil, and capers. Continue stirring and add the red pepper flakes, pepper, and parsley.

Cook for no longer than 18 minutes. Cook linguine al dente and toss with the sauce. *Serves 4.*

GROUND VEAL
WITH SPINACH NOODLES

1 small onion, minced
4 tablespoons olive oil
8 ounces ground veal
1 cup chopped plum tomatoes
4 ounces spinach, chopped
4 tablespoons grated Parmesan cheese
$^1/_2$ teaspoon dried sage
Freshly ground black pepper to taste
$^3/_4$ pound green fettuccine

Sauté the onion in olive oil until soft. Add the veal and brown; discard any excess fat. Add the tomatoes, spinach, grated Parmesan, sage, and pepper. Cover and simmer 25 to 30 minutes.

Meanwhile, cook the fettuccine al dente. Spoon the sauce over the cooked pasta and serve. *Serves 4.*

EGGS

Always purchase eggs that have been refrigerated. Keep eggs covered in the refrigerator to maintain their quality longer.

My grandmother always told me that if there were a few eggs in my refrigerator, I could put together a meal in no time. How right she was.

Take a potato, an onion, some leftover vegetables, maybe even some cooked meat or chicken, a pinch of this and a pinch of that, and in a short time you can make a delicious Italian omelette called a frittata. It is better than a deep-dish pizza.

You can use other vegetables in the recipe below, but here is a combination that works well.

VEGETABLE-CHEESE FRITTATA

3 medium red potatoes, skins on, preboiled and sliced
   thick
1 red bell pepper, cored, seeded, and diced
1 medium onion, thinly sliced
3 tablespoons olive oil
3 tablespoons unsalted butter
8 eggs
1 cup shredded Jarlsberg cheese
1/2 teaspoon dried thyme
Freshly ground pepper to taste

Sauté the potatoes, pepper, and onion in olive oil and butter in large 10-inch skillet or nonstick pan until the onion is translucent.

Beat the eggs until frothy; add the cheese, thyme, and pepper to the eggs. Pour the mixture evenly into the skillet and shake it into place.

When the bottom is formed and browned, put a large plate over the pan, flip, then slide the frittata back into the pan to cook the top. If you do not feel confident enough to do this, put the pan under the broiler for 3 to 4 minutes. *Serves 4 to 6.*

FRENCH MUSHROOM OMELETTE

Don't be intimidated by omelettes. After you make a couple of these, you will be a pro and will create some interesting fillings of your own.

6 eggs
6 tablespoons milk
Freshly ground pepper to taste
Pinch of salt
3 tablespoons unsalted butter
1 tablespoon Dijon mustard
1 cup sliced mushrooms lightly sautéed in
    ½ tablespoon butter
Optional:
Cooked diced ham, cooked crumbled bacon, pimento

Combine the eggs with the milk, pepper, and salt, and beat lightly. In your favorite omelette pan, melt the butter. Pour the eggs into the pan. Scatter your choice of fillings on the eggs, in the center. As the eggs set on the outer edges of the pan, use a fork and draw them toward the center of the pan. Repeat and shake the pan to allow the uncooked liquid to set and cook. Repeat until the egg almost forms a large pancake. Spoon the mustard into the center of the omelette, and spread the mushrooms on top. With a spatula, lift up and fold. When the omelette sets, slide it onto a serving dish; fold a second time if desired. *Serves 2.*

EGG FOO YUNG

These little individual Chinese omelettes are quick to make.

6 eggs
Dash of salt
Freshly ground pepper to taste
2 cups bean sprouts, preferably fresh
Oil
1/2 cup chopped scallions
Soy sauce
Hot pepper sauce
Optional:
1 cup cooked chopped ham, turkey, or chicken

In a bowl, beat the eggs with the salt and pepper, then add the sprouts. In a lightly oiled 6-inch skillet, sauté the scallions until they are translucent, about 6 minutes. Add the scallions to the egg mixture. Add your choice of meat.

Brush oil on a skillet (unless it is a nonstick pan) and when it is hot, add one-quarter of the egg mixture. Brown on one side, flip over, and brown the other side. Repeat for 4 servings. Serve with soy sauce and hot pepper sauce on the side. *Serves 4.*

OLD-COUNTRY QUICHE

2 potatoes, thinly sliced
1 onion, thinly sliced
2 tablespoons unsalted butter
3 eggs, lightly beaten
1 cup light cream
$^1/_2$ cup grated Gruyère cheese
3 tablespoons Dijon mustard
Freshly ground pepper to taste
Salt, if desired
1 lightly baked 9-inch pie shell, firm but not brown

Preheat oven to 375°F.

In a skillet, sauté the potatoes and onion in the butter until cooked and lightly browned, about 18 to 20 minutes. Cool slightly.

Mix the eggs, cream, Gruyère, mustard, pepper, and salt if desired into the potato-onion mixture. Pour into the pre-baked pie shell. Bake in oven 35 to 40 minutes, or until knife inserted into center comes out clean. Cool slightly before cutting. *Serves 4 to 6.*

GROUND MEAT

I never cared much for meat loaves and their dubious ingredients. But discussing ground meat recipes with old kitchen hands, one discovers the myriad of hand-me-down favorites like Monday Meat Loaf, Hobo Special, Chilli-Willi, Working Girls' Casserole, and Single-Again Special, to mention a few.

Ground beef, veal, pork, and turkey are widely available in most markets. If you have a food processor, it can process meat to a fine consistency.

It is probably safe to say that every American over the age of six has had a traditional hamburger—bun and burger with ketchup. Everyone has his or her own idea of how to make and season burgers. Some add raw onions, onion soup mix, ketchup, Worcestershire sauce, and/or pepper to the meat before cooking. Try variations that you feel mix well with the beef.

Today most of us use a leaner meat for burgers. Because of this, I add 1 beaten egg white per pound of beef to make the burgers fluffier, and 1 or 2 tablespoons of Worcestershire sauce for flavor. When you cook hamburgers on the griddle or in a frying pan, don't try to flatten them with your spatula. If you do, you will have flat, dry burgers instead of thick, juicy ones.

VEAL AND LIMA BEAN CASSEROLE

1 cup dried baby lima beans
2 tablespoons unsalted butter
1 pound ground veal
1/2 cup finely chopped onion
1 green bell pepper, diced
2 cups tomato sauce
Dash of garlic powder
1/2 teaspoon cumin
1 bay leaf
1 tablespoon sugar
2 pinches of oregano
Freshly ground pepper to taste
Salt, if desired
1 1/2 cups shredded Jarlsberg cheese
Paprika

Wash and soak the dried beans overnight. Cook the beans in a covered saucepan with fresh water to cover; simmer until the beans are tender, about 1 hour. Drain and set aside.

Preheat the oven to 350°F.

Melt 1 tablespoon butter and lightly brown the veal, onion, and bell pepper. Remove the veal and vegetables and set aside.

Discard any fat in the pan. Add the tomato sauce, garlic powder, cumin, bay leaf, sugar, oregano, pepper, and salt if desired, and simmer 10 to 12 minutes.

Generously butter an ovenproof casserole with the remaining butter. Make alternate layers of sauce, veal, beans, and cheese. Finish with a sprinkling of paprika on top. Cook, covered, in the oven for about 1 hour. *Serves 4 to 6.*

GRANDMA'S MEAT LOAF

When Grandma made meat loaf, I was always at her door. This is easy and delicious—your basic meat loaf. Cold, it is good for sandwiches. You may want to double this recipe for leftovers.

1 pound lean ground beef
$\frac{1}{2}$ cup bread crumbs
2 egg whites, beaten
1 egg yolk
1 small onion, minced
1 cup tomato sauce, or $\frac{1}{2}$ cup tomato ketchup
(Grandma never used ketchup)
1 tablespoon Worcestershire sauce
2 pinches of dried thyme
Freshly ground pepper to taste
Salt, if desired

Preheat the oven to 350°F.

Mix the meat with the other ingredients in a large bowl. Pack the mixture into a greased loaf pan. (If you put a piece of lightly greased doubled aluminum foil in the bottom of the pan, longer in length than the pan, it will be easier to remove the loaf.)

Cook in the oven for approximately 50 minutes to 1 hour. *Serves 4.*

MOM'S MEATBALLS

1 pound ground beef
2 cloves garlic, minced
2 eggs
$1/2$ cup chopped Italian parsley
$1/2$ cup grated Parmesan cheese
$3/4$ cup fine bread crumbs
$1/2$ teaspoon oregano
Freshly ground pepper to taste
Salt, if desired
2 tablespoons olive oil

Mix the beef with all the other ingredients except the olive oil. Form the mixture into approximately 8 meatballs of 3 ounces each.

If you are planning to serve them in a tomato sauce such as the Marinara Sauce on page 58, brown them lightly in oil for a few minutes, then put them into the simmering sauce and cook until the sauce is done.

If you are serving them without a sauce, brown them in oil in a covered pan for 2 to 3 minutes. Turn the meatballs and cook for another 2 minutes or more. Remove with slotted spoon and drain on paper towels. *Serves 4.*

SHEPHERD'S PIE

After sipping a few stouts in a London pub, this tasted delicious!

1 pound ground beef
1 small onion, chopped
1 tablespoon olive oil
1 teaspoon Worcestershire sauce
1 cup fresh or thawed frozen peas
1 carrot, sliced and partially cooked
$1/2$ teaspoon dried thyme
1 teaspoon sage
Freshly ground pepper to taste
Salt, if desired
3 large potatoes, cooked and mashed
4 tablespoons unsalted butter
Up to $1/2$ cup milk

Preheat oven to 375°F.

Sauté the beef and onion in the olive oil until lightly browned. Drain off excess fat and add the Worcestershire sauce.

Place the mixture in a greased baking dish. Add the peas and carrot, and sprinkle with thyme, sage, pepper, and salt, if desired. Mash potatoes with 2 tablespoons butter and milk, and add salt and pepper if desired. Place mashed potatoes on top of beef mixture and dot with remaining butter. Cook in oven approximately 30 minutes, until browned on top and heated through. *Serves 2.*

SKILLET LAMB

1 pound ground lamb
2 tablespoons olive oil
1 clove garlic
1 small onion, sliced
1 cup tomato sauce or Marinara Sauce (see p. 58)
1 medium eggplant, skin on, cubed (4 cups)
6 to 8 large green olives, sliced
$1/2$ teaspoon dried thyme
Approximately $1/2$ teaspoon dried basil
1 tablespoon grated Parmesan cheese
Freshly ground pepper to taste
Salt to taste
$1/2$ cup grated mozzarella or Jarlsberg cheese

In a large skillet, lightly brown the lamb in oil. Remove the lamb and sauté the garlic and onion in the drippings until the onion is translucent. Discard the garlic and excess fat.

Add the tomato sauce, eggplant, olives, thyme, basil, Parmesan cheese, pepper, and salt to the skillet. Cover and simmer 30 minutes, or until tender.

Add the lamb and cook an additional 10 to 15 minutes, uncovered. Turn off the heat.

Sprinkle the grated mozzarella or Jarlsberg cheese over the top of the lamb mixture and cover the pan. When the cheese melts, it is ready to serve. *Serves 4.*

IV.
One-Dish Meals

❖

Ham Rollups

Chili con Carne: Francis's Creative Can-Opener Meal

Chicken Corsica

Chicken and Peppers, Roman Style

Top-of-Stove Cassoulet

Lamb Stew

Ginger Shrimp and Broccoli Stir-Fry

Scallops à la Kathie Lee

Island Seafood Sauté

Lobster

❖

One-dish meals like casseroles, skillet dinners, and pot-au-feu are great answers to less fuss and no muss. Rounded out by a fresh green salad and some bread, you have a nutritious and balanced meal.

You must be careful, however, because if canned soups are the basis for the casserole recipes, these one-dish casseroles become dumping grounds for excess sodium and preservatives. This is the main reason you rarely see me use canned soups when I cook on television or at personal appearances. But I do realize that many Americans utilize these products as budget extenders for feeding a large family or utilizing leftovers. And I am all for shortcuts; as a matter of fact, my chili recipe in this chapter uses canned soups, as do some of my quick-sauce ideas made with soups (see page 97). Just be sure to take particular care to buy soups with the lowest sodium content.

Stews are an obvious one-dish meal and they are really simple to make and economical. You can utilize the more inexpensive cuts of meat, since they will become tender when stewed, hence the label "stewing meat." Double some of these recipes and freeze them for another time. When reheating, add vegetables, like peas, pea pods, and green beans, that do not require a long cooking time. See the two beef stews on pages 36–38.

There are myriad chili recipes and, of course, every one is the best of its kind. I have participated in chili cookoffs and tasted regional chili from the famous Cincinnati Chili to Texas and Albuquerque renditions. I am sure your own recipe collection has a few favorites, some hot, some mild. I think you will like mine. It was an instant favorite that fed hundreds at an Italian food fair in the Meadowlands in New Jersey in 1979.

Fresh breads and salads are the perfect accompaniments for a one-dish meal. Do not restrict yourself to iceberg lettuce from the head lettuce family. Here are a few leafy alternatives that make salads interesting:

Leaf lettuce grows in bunches rather than from heads. The soft and tender leaves vary in color from yellowish to green to red. Romaine has a distinctive flavor, more pronounced than iceberg it is the only lettuce used in Caesar salad. Bibb lettuce has a soft, delicate leaf with a sweet flavor. It lends contrast to other greens when added to your salad bowl. Boston lettuce, also known as butterhead, has a light green leaf with a delicate flavor. Escarole is the most bitter of the greens, so it is ideal to mix with some of these other lettuces. Chicory is also bitter when eaten raw; when it is cooked with garlic and oil, it becomes a delicious hot vegetable.

I wash and dry various kinds of lettuce and mix them together. Store the greens in a plastic bag in the refrigerator. When preparing a meal, the salad is ready to be laid into a dish and dressed. Make up a jar of your own dressing or try my All-Purpose Vinaigrette Salad Dressing (page 25). Experiment with different vinegars and flavor your olive oils with garlic, pepper pods, and sprigs of fresh herbs. I prefer olive oil because the taste is flavor-enhancing rather than totally neutral, and the health benefits are a plus. Olive oil is beneficial in the overall battle against bad cholesterol.

HAM ROLLUPS

I was getting this recipe together for the "Morning Show" in Houston in 1982, when a guy walked up to me and said hi. Normally I introduce myself, but since I was running a little late with my preparation, I excused myself and invited him back later to taste the recipe with the crew. It turned out to be Lee Greenwood, who won the Country Music Award that evening, and later he did indeed join the crew for dinner.

1 small onion, minced
4 tablespoons unsalted butter or margarine
1 cup water
One 16-ounce can Bartlett pears, chopped, 3/4 cup
    juice reserved
1 1/2 cups seasoned bread stuffing
1/8 teaspoon allspice
1/8 teaspoon dry mustard
4 ounces pear schnapps liqueur
8 small or 4 large slices of boiled ham sliced about
    1/16 inch thick

Sauté the onion in 2 tablespoons butter or margarine. Add the water, chopped pears, reserved pear juice, and bread stuffing. After 5 minutes, remove the stuffing from the pan and set aside.

To the same pan, add the remaining 2 tablespoons butter or margarine, the allspice, mustard, and pear schnapps. Mix well and add ham slices.

Brown the ham slices on both sides for 2 to 3 minutes total cooking time, and remove to a separate plate. Fill each slice with the stuffing mixture. Roll up the ham, fastening each bundle with toothpicks, if necessary.

Continue to cook the sauce until it thickens, then pour over the ham. *Serves 4.*

CHILI CON CARNE
Francis's Creative Can-Opener Meal

This is great for a party, is very quick and easy to make ahead, and freezes perfectly. Serve with bowls of plain boiled white rice, and pass around a bowl of grated Cheddar cheese for topping, if you wish. Here's how I do it, my way.

2 pounds chuck steak
1 tablespoon flour
4 tablespoons olive oil
1 large onion, sliced
$3/4$ cup red wine
1 cup tomato sauce
1 clove garlic, pressed
1 carrot, cut into matchsticks
1 green bell pepper, diced
One 20-ounce can or two $10^{1/2}$-ounce cans kidney
   beans, drained
One 20-ounce can or two $10^{1/2}$-ounce cans chick-peas,
   drained

One 10½-ounce can minestrone soup
One 10½-ounce can lentil soup
2 bay leaves
½ teaspoon cumin
1 teaspoon oregano
¼ teaspoon crushed red pepper flakes (more or less
    to taste)
Freshly ground pepper to taste
Optional:
Grated Cheddar cheese

Cut the steak into thin strips and sprinkle with flour. In
a very large skillet, heat 2 tablespoons oil. Sauté the onion
slices in the oil; remove the onion and set aside. Quickly
brown the meat in the hot oil. You will need to do this in 2
batches, using the remaining oil for the second batch.

Add ¼ cup wine, scraping ingredients from the bottom
of the pan and stirring. Add the tomato sauce, the onion, the
rest of the wine, and all other ingredients. Taste and adjust
seasoning.

Cover and cook over low heat for approximately 1½
hours or until the meat is tender. Uncover for the last 30
minutes if the sauce needs thickening. *Serves 8.*

CHICKEN CORSICA

Mustard greens, often available in frozen form in the supermarket, give a strong, bitter taste that blends in nicely with the other flavors in this chicken casserole. You can substitute collard greens or spinach, but the taste will not be the same.

I make this recipe with dried white beans that require presoaking before cooking, but if you are in a rush, you can use canned white cannellini beans. If you do, cut the chicken stock to less than half a cup and add it and the beans to the casserole for the last 40 minutes of cooking.

1 chicken, cut into serving-size pieces
2 tablespoons olive oil
1 large onion, sliced
1 ¼-inch-thick slice cooked ham, diced
1 cup chopped plum tomatoes
1 cup dried white kidney beans, pre-soaked and
    drained or one 19-ounce can cannellini (cooked
    white kidney beans), rinsed and drained
10 to 12 ounces chopped mustard greens, fresh
    or frozen
½-1 cup chicken stock
1 dozen large green olives, cut into quarters
½ teaspoon dried rosemary
¼ teaspoon dried marjoram
1 tablespoon lemon juice
½ teaspoon sugar
Freshly ground pepper to taste
Salt, if desired

Wash the chicken pieces and pat them dry. Heat the oil in a large skillet or stove-top casserole. Brown the chicken pieces and remove to a separate plate. Pour off all but one or two tablespoons fat.

Sauté the onion and ham briefly and return the chicken to the pan. Add the tomatoes, beans, mustard greens, and chicken stock. Cover the pan and cook over medium heat for about 20 minutes.

Add the olives, rosemary, marjoram, lemon juice, sugar, pepper, and salt if desired. Cover the pan and continue cooking for another 30 to 40 minutes. *Serves 4.*

CHICKEN AND PEPPERS, ROMAN STYLE

One 3- to 3 1/2-pound chicken, cut up
1 clove garlic, peeled
1/2 medium onion, chopped
3 ounces olive oil
1 tablespoon unsalted butter
1 pound small potatoes scrubbed, skins on, quartered
One 16-ounce can Italian plum tomatoes, drained
1 pound green bell peppers, cored, seeded, and cut
    lengthwise into 2-inch strips
2 bay leaves
Dash of thyme
1/2 teaspoon crushed hot red pepper flakes
Salt, if desired
Freshly ground pepper to taste

Wash the chicken pieces and pat them dry. Gently sauté the garlic and onion in oil and butter until they turn a golden brown. Discard the garlic.

Add the cut-up chicken to the pan, and brown it on all sides. Add the potatoes, tomatoes, and bell peppers. Add the bay leaves, thyme, hot pepper, salt if desired, and pepper.

Cover and simmer about 40 minutes. If there is too much liquid, remove the cover of the pan and cook uncovered for the last 15 minutes. *Serves 4 to 6.*

TOP-OF-STOVE CASSOULET

1 pound boneless lamb, cut into 1-inch cubes
$^1/_2$ pound sweet Italian sausage, sliced bite-size
1 onion, chopped
3 tablespoons olive oil
1 $^1/_2$ cups tomato sauce
2 cups cooked white beans (freshly cooked or canned
    and drained)
$^1/_2$ cup red wine
1 bay leaf
$^1/_2$ teaspoon savory
Freshly ground pepper to taste
Salt, if desired

Sauté the lamb, sausage, and onion in the olive oil until the lamb is brown. Drain off the excess fat and add the remaining ingredients.

Cover and simmer about 1 $^1/_2$ hours, stirring occasionally. *Serves 4.*

LAMB STEW

2 tablespoons olive oil
1 clove garlic, minced
2 pounds lamb shoulder or boneless lamb for stew, cut
  into 1-inch cubes
$1/2$ teaspoon rosemary
$1/2$ teaspoon dried thyme
Freshly ground pepper to taste
Salt, if desired
2 cups water
1 cup beef stock
1 cup dry red wine
6 to 8 carrots, peeled and cut into chunks
4 small whole onions, peeled and quartered
4 ribs celery, cut into pieces
2 to 3 medium potatoes, sliced with skins
2 tablespoons flour dissolved in 3 tablespoons water
2 tablespoons chopped fresh parsley

In a large Dutch oven, heat the oil and add the garlic.
Sauté garlic for 1 minute, then add the meat and brown on
all sides in the hot oil. Add the rosemary, thyme, pepper, salt
if desired, water, beef stock, and red wine. Cover the pan and
simmer 45 minutes to 1 hour, stirring occasionally.

Add the vegetables. Cover and cook 30 minutes longer,
or until the meat and vegetables are tender.

Add the flour and water mixture to thicken the stew.
Taste and add additional seasonings, if desired. Sprinkle with
chopped parsley. *Serves 6.*

GINGER SHRIMP AND BROCCOLI STIR-FRY

12 to 16 large shrimps
1 head broccoli
2 tablespoons peanut oil
2 scallions, chopped
1 clove garlic
$1/2$ teaspoon finely grated fresh ginger
2 tablespoons medium-dry sherry
1 tablespoon soy sauce
2 large red bell peppers, cored, seeded, and cut into
  strips
1 teaspoon cornstarch dissolved in 1 tablespoon cold
  water

Rinse, peel, and devein the shrimp. Cut the broccoli into small florets and thinly slice the large stem. Heat the oil in a large skillet or wok. Add the scallions, garlic, ginger, and broccoli, and quickly stir-fry for 2 to 3 minutes.

Add the sherry and soy sauce and continue to cook, stirring, for approximately 3 to 4 minutes. Add the peppers and shrimp, reduce the heat, and cook, covered, for an additional 3 to 4 minutes. Remove the cover, add the cornstarch mixture, and stir until thickened. *Serves 4.*

SCALLOPS À LA KATHIE LEE

I named this dish in honor of Kathie Lee Gifford when we celebrated her birthday on "Live with Regis and Kathie Lee."

1 pound scallops
1 medium onion, sliced
2 cloves garlic, chopped
$1/4$ cup olive oil
2 tablespoons unsalted butter
4 to 6 ripe plum tomatoes, sliced
$1/2$ carrot, cut into thin julienne sticks
4 ounces thin spaghetti, broken into 1-inch pieces
1 tablespoon oyster or soy sauce
4 fresh basil leaves
$1/4$ teaspoon dry mustard
Freshly ground pepper to taste
Salt, if desired
1 tablespoon water

Rinse and dry the scallops. If you are using sea scallops, cut them into quarters.

Sauté the onion and garlic in the olive oil and butter until soft. Add the tomatoes, carrot, spaghetti pieces, and oyster or soy sauce. Season with the basil, mustard, pepper, and salt if desired. Add the water. Cover and let simmer 5 to 8 minutes.

Place the scallops on top of the mixture and cook, covered, for another 4 to 5 minutes. *Serves 4.*

ISLAND SEAFOOD SAUTÉ

$^{1}/_{3}$ cup olive oil
1 pound firm-flesh fish, such as cod, scrod, grouper, or
   snapper, cut in large chunks
$^{1}/_{2}$ pound fresh mushrooms, thinly sliced (2 cups)
1 red bell pepper, cut into strips (1 cup)
$^{1}/_{2}$ cup thinly sliced celery
$^{1}/_{2}$ cup sliced scallions
1 clove garlic, minced
One 8-ounce can water chestnuts, drained and sliced
$^{1}/_{2}$ cup coconut rum liqueur
2 tablespoons soy sauce
1 tablespoon cornstarch

In a large skillet, heat the oil and sauté the fish on all sides until it is cooked and flaky, about 3 minutes. Remove the fish and set aside.

In the same skillet, stir-fry the mushrooms, bell pepper, celery, scallions, garlic, and water chestnuts about 3 minutes, until the vegetables are crisp but tender.

In a small bowl, mix the coconut rum liqueur, soy sauce, and cornstarch; add this mixture to the vegetables, stirring constantly, until the mixture thickens. Return the fish to the skillet and mix gently into the vegetables. Cook just long enough to heat the fish. *Serves 4.*

LOBSTER

Lobsters are really easy one-dish meals, and thanks to sea-food departments in most supermarkets you can buy them everywhere. A great simple salad and a basket of sourdough rolls are all you will need for this easy feast. The delicious sweet taste of the meat shouldn't be masked by other flavors. Well, butter or lemon juice, if you must! Many people prefer small lobsters because they claim the meat is more tender and sweeter than the meat in large lobsters over 3 pounds. I proved that old wives' tale totally wrong by giving a wildly successful lobster feast where ten guests shared one 16-pound lobster.

Coral or roe, a small pink mass, is found only in female lobsters. The coral and the green tomalley, the liver, may be eaten; both are considered great delicacies.

Be sure you buy lobsters that are alive and kicking. Keep them in a bag in the refrigerator before cooking. You may feel squeamish about killing the lobsters, but by following these simple directions, you will find it is not hard. The most popular methods for cooking lobsters are steaming, boiling, broiling, and barbecuing.

To Boil Lobsters

If the lobsters are 1 1/4 to 1 1/2 pounds, plunge them head-first into a large pot filled with rapidly boiling water. Cover the pot, and when the water comes up to the boil again, cook about 10 minutes. For a 2-pound lobster cook 5 minutes longer. You may want to hold the top of the pot on with your hand or weight it with something for the first few minutes of cooking, because lobsters flick their tails when they first hit the boiling water and can send the top flying across the room.

If you are cooking a very large lobster, or a number of lobsters for a crowd, be sure you have a large enough pot to hold them comfortably. If you don't, ask your fishmonger to cook them for you.

To Steam Lobsters

Place a steamer rack on the bottom of a large pan with about 1 1/2 inches of boiling water. Place live lobsters on the rack, cover the pan, and cook until the shells are red, approximately 18 minutes.

To clean and open boiled or steamed lobsters for serving, follow instructions for killing a lobster for broiling or barbecuing that follow.

To Kill a Lobster for Broiling or Barbecuing

Lay the live lobster on a table on its back, holding it down firmly with one hand (wrapped in a towel or oven mitt). Plunge a large, heavy knife into the head, and press the knife firmly down to split the lobster meat in two from head to tail, being careful not to cut through the back shell. Remove and discard the sac or stomach near the back of the head and the intestinal vein, a long white strip along the length of the tail meat.

Lobsters are great on the grill too! Preparing lobsters to cook under the broiler or on the barbecue is essentially the same process.

To Barbecue

Open and clean 1¼- to 1½-pound lobsters as described above. Brush the meat with olive oil. Place the lobsters, meat side down, on the grill, not too close to the heat. If you are using a gas or electric grill, set the heat between low and medium. If your grill has a hood, close it and cook the lobsters for about 5 minutes. Flip the lobsters over and continue to cook with the hood down for another 4 minutes or longer. The shells will turn red. Cooking time is dependent on the intensity of the fire. Serve with lemon juice or butter.

To Oven-Broil

Brush the lobster meat with olive oil and place on broiler pan, meat side down. Cook about 5 minutes. Turn over to finish cooking meat side up. Check carefully to be sure meat does not overcook.

V.
Seasonal Cooking

SAUCES

Herbed Sauce
Summer Dressing
Brandy Mayonnaise
A Sauce for All Seasons

❖

SOUPS

Basic Chicken Stock
Turkey Soup
Cousin Paula's Soup
Pumpkin Soup
Black Bean Soup
Down-Home Split-Pea Soup
"A Touch of Spring" Soup
Gazpacho

❖

WINTER NIGHT SUPPER

Anywhere, U.S.A. Goulash

❖

SUMMER NIGHT SUPPER

Cape Cod Fish Stew

❖

Today we see fruits and vegetables virtually year-round in the supermarket. If you are willing to pay the tariff, you can have fresh asparagus or nectarines anytime of the year. It is wiser to take advantage of the peak vegetable-growing seasons by freezing as much as you can store.

Frozen vegetables are always preferable over canned. Most processors process and flash-freeze produce within hours of harvesting, assuring you of maximum flavor and vitamin retention. So if you see fresh produce that is tired from its long journey to you or worn out by improper handling, it is better to choose frozen items.

In the warm seasons, when vegetables are plentiful, experiment with different herbs and vegetable combinations. Try basil with turnips, squash, beans, and spinach. When boiling potatoes or rice or beets, add a bay leaf. Caraway seeds are delicious with cauliflower. (To keep cauliflower snowy white, add ½ cup milk to the cooking water.) Caraway is also good with turnips and with that all-time favorite, cabbage and sauerkraut.

Dill perks up the taste of lima beans and beets, as does marjoram with carrots, tomatoes, and peas. Freshly grated nutmeg is so much better than ground nutmeg in a jar, it is worth your while to buy one of those little nutmeg grinders and whole nutmegs. Grate some on kale, peas, broccoli, and limas for a different taste.

Tarragon lovers should try fresh tarragon with lettuce, asparagus, peas, and spinach. Thyme and oregano are used in many recipes with tomatoes and eggplant. Try them with a beet salad for light summer dining.

I recommend steaming vegetables or cooking them completely waterless. The old-fashioned practice of immersing vegetables in large quantities of boiling water, which is then thrown out after the cooking, has made the kitchen sink one of the healthiest members of the American family, because down the drain goes much of the vitamins, minerals, and flavor of the vegetables.

In my family, when Mom boiled spinach she made my brother and me drink big glasses of the spinach water. Of course we hated it, but Mom knew the water was good. Even potato skins used to be thrown away and now, of course, they are popular and appear on many menus served in a variety of ways. I have been saying for a long time that you should always use the potato skin, even for mashed potatoes and fried potatoes. The mineral salts and lots of flavor are right under the skin.

Tender corn on the cob is so much more delicious when it is not boiled to death. Husk the corn and remove the silk. Wash the leaves and corn in cold water. Do not shake off excess water. Layer the bottom of a large 12- to 14-inch skillet outfitted with a tight-fitting lid with some of the leaves. Place a layer of the washed corn on the leaves and cover with some more leaves. Cover the pan and cook on high heat until the lid is hot to the touch—not long. Lower to a simmer and, if no steam escapes, you will have luscious corn in about 18 minutes. When I cook corn I sprinkle some ground coriander on it, which highlights the sweetness. Thus, you can avoid salt or butter if you choose.

Try carrots my way. It is very important to use a pan with a tight-fitting cover. Peel and wash the carrots and put them into your pan with no oil or butter, and cover. Use high heat until the lid is hot to the touch, reduce to simmer, and in about 12 to 15 minutes your carrots will be delicious and sweet all by themselves. Did you ever wonder why carrot cake tastes so good? Cook carrots a little longer than usual and you will see sugar oozing out and caramelizing in the pan.

When it's hot—keep it cool! Many creative cooks lose their creativity when it gets hot outdoors and too hot in the kitchen. Sometimes shortcuts are in order. For instance, you need a quick sauce to perk up some vegetables or a cold chicken or turkey? Well, okay, I won't look. Heat a can of Cheddar cheese soup and add a couple dashes of hot pepper sauce and about $1/4$ teaspoon cayenne pepper for a spicy cheese sauce.

To a can of cream of mushroom soup, add $1/2$ cup chopped mushrooms and 1 teaspoon tarragon for instant hot chicken gravy. You can make a quick tasty sauce by mixing either cream of mushroom or cream of celery soup with $1/4$ cup mayonnaise and 3 teaspoons lemon juice. Of course, these are substitutes for the real thing, but handy when you are simply not in the mood to start from scratch.

SAUCES

HERBED SAUCE

Here's a sauce to keep on hand for those lazy, hazy days of summer. It is great on cold turkey or chicken. If you are watching your weight or your cholesterol, use a diet or light mayonnaise.

1 cup mayonnaise
$^1/_2$ cup white wine
$^1/_2$ cup chopped fresh parsley
2 teaspoons crushed fresh tarragon
Dash of chervil
1 small onion, minced
1 clove garlic, crushed
Generous amount of freshly ground pepper

Whisk all ingredients together. Cover and refrigerate several hours before using. It will keep a week or two in the refrigerator. *Makes 2 cups.*

SUMMER DRESSING

I like to serve this sauce in a small cup in the center of a bountiful plate of blanched summer vegetables and a couple of breadsticks.

8 ounces plain yogurt
$1/2$ cup mayonnaise
2 tablespoons chili sauce
1 tablespoon grated onion
1 teaspoon tarragon vinegar
$1/4$ teaspoon curry powder
$1/8$ teaspoon ground thyme

Stir together all ingredients. Cover and chill. It will keep about 4 days to a week in the refrigerator. *Makes about 1$3/4$ cups.*

BRANDY MAYONNAISE

This is a deliciously different cocktail sauce for cold shrimp, crab, lobster, or salmon.

1 cup mayonnaise
1 tablespoon sour cream
$1/4$ teaspoon dried dill
1 teaspoon fresh lemon juice
1 teaspoon Dijon mustard
4 tablespoons brandy

Blend all ingredients well. Cover and chill at least one hour before serving to enhance flavor. This will keep about a week in the refrigerator. *Makes 1 $1/4$ cups.*

A SAUCE FOR ALL SEASONS

Serve this as a condiment on cooked fish, chicken, or rice, or add a few drops when grilling or broiling fish.

1 cup low-sodium soy sauce
One 1-inch cube ginger root, thinly sliced
3 cloves garlic, pressed
2 tablespoons fresh lemon juice
1 tablespoon white distilled vinegar
1 1/2 tablespoons sugar
1/2 cup water
2 dashes bitters
2 dashes hot pepper sauce

Place all the ingredients in a saucepan and bring to a boil. Remove from heat. Let cool and pour into a jar with cover. Store in refrigerator. It keeps for a long time. *Makes 1 3/4 cups.*

SOUPS

BASIC CHICKEN STOCK

I always keep this tasty, rich stock in my freezer. Use it to flavor the cooking water for rice, for steaming vegetables, and as the base for soups, stews, et cetera.

If you do not plan to use all the stock within two days, freeze it. You might find it convenient, as I do, to use an ice cube tray for just this purpose. Cover the tray with plastic wrap until frozen. Remove the cubes to a plastic bag and store them in the freezer.

3 pounds chicken, cut up
$4^1/_2$ quarts fresh cold water
2 large carrots, peeled or scrubbed
2 ribs celery
3 medium onions, peeled
2 bay leaves
1 tablespoon whole peppercorns
$^1/_2$ teaspoon dried marjoram
$^1/_2$ teaspoon dried thyme
Salt, if desired

Wash the chicken parts and place them in a large pan and cover with the cold water. Coarsely cut up the vegetables and add to the pot. Add the bay leaves, peppercorns, marjoram, thyme, and salt if desired.

Cover and bring to a boil, then lower heat to a simmer. Occasionally skim off any foam residue. Continue to cook at a slow simmer, covered, for about 2½ to 3 hours. Remove the cover and simmer an additional hour to concentrate all the flavors. Add boiling water if the stock level gets too low.

Strain the stock and defat. Remove the tenderest chicken meat, discard the skin and bones. Freeze the meat for use in other recipes. *Makes 2 quarts.*

TURKEY SOUP

Consider all the different recipes we have seen that included leftover turkey meat (see index). Now the bones are going to make one of the best soups; that's getting your money's worth and then some. I like to make enough soup to allow for more on other winter nights.

> 1 whole turkey carcass, with leftover bones but no
>   skin
> 6 quarts fresh cold water
> 1 medium onion, chopped
> 4 ribs celery, sliced
> 2 parsnips, peeled and cut into 1-inch pieces
> One 28-ounce can stewed tomatoes with juice
> 1 teaspoon poultry seasoning
> Salt, if desired
> Freshly ground pepper to taste
> 1 teaspoon lemon juice
> $^1/_2$ cup uncooked white rice

Place the turkey bones in your largest pot; add the water, cover, and bring to a boil. Then lower the heat to a simmer, occasionally skimming off any foam residue.

Continue to cook at a slow simmer, covered, for about 2 to $2^1/_2$ hours.

Strain and defat stock, and return it to the pan. Your stock should be reduced by a quart or so; if not, boil it for several minutes more to reduce.

The bones and the meat must now be carefully separated. Discard all bones, making sure you find the small bone pieces. Put the meat back into the stock with the onion, celery, and parsnips. Add the tomatoes and their juice, the seasonings, and lemon juice. Return to a boil; then lower to a simmer and cook uncovered. Do not add any additional water during cooking. Cook an additional 45 minutes.

Add the rice and cook another 45 minutes to 1 hour. *Makes approximately 3¹/₂ to 4 quarts.*

COUSIN PAULA'S SOUP

8 ounces kale
8 ounces mushrooms
4 medium red potatoes
2 quarts chicken stock
1 clove garlic, peeled
2 teaspoons summer savory
1 teaspoon marjoram
Juice of 1 lemon
1 teaspoon Dijon mustard
Freshly ground pepper to taste
Salt, if desired

Wash and coarsely chop the kale. Cut the mushrooms and potatoes into small pieces. Bring the chicken stock to a boil, then add the kale, potatoes, mushrooms, and all the seasonings.

When the vegetables are tender, about 15 minutes, remove them to a food processor or blender and purée. Return the purée to the stock and mix well. Serve hot. *Serves 8 to 10.*

PUMPKIN SOUP

6 shallots, peeled and chopped
2 tablespoons unsalted butter
3 cups chicken stock
$^1/_2$ cup *acini pepe* pasta (very small, resembles rice)
1 $^1/_2$ cups canned pumpkin
$^1/_2$ cup light cream
3 tablespoons grated Parmesan cheese
$^1/_3$ cup chopped fresh dill
$^1/_2$ teaspoon dry mustard
Freshly ground pepper to taste
Salt, if desired

Sweat the shallots in the butter for a few minutes. Add the chicken stock, bring to a boil, and add the pasta. Continue to cook about 5 minutes.

Stir in the pumpkin, cream, and grated Parmesan. Reduce the heat to a simmer, and add the dill, mustard, pepper, and salt if desired. Continue to cook over low heat about 25 minutes. Serve hot. *Serves 6 to 8.*

BLACK BEAN SOUP

There is something about this soup and the following split-pea soup that warms you quickly even when the temperature outside is below freezing.

1 cup dried black beans
2 quarts beef stock
2 bay leaves
$^1/_2$ cup chopped fresh coriander, reserving
   1 tablespoon for garnish
Freshly ground pepper to taste
1 $^1/_2$ onions, chopped
2 cloves garlic, peeled
1 cup tomato sauce
2 tablespoons unsalted butter, if desired
$^1/_2$ cup sour cream for garnish

Soak the beans in water overnight.

Put the beef stock and drained beans in a large saucepan over medium heat. Add the bay leaves, coriander, and pepper. Add 1 chopped onion (reserve $^1/_2$ onion for garnish), the garlic cloves, and the tomato sauce.

Bring to a boil, reduce heat to a simmer, cover, and cook about 1$^1/_2$ hours, stirring occasionally. Add butter, if desired, for extra flavor. Continue to cook, uncovered, about 1 to 1$^1/_2$ hours, depending on desired thickness of the soup.

Garnish soup with a dollop of sour cream, chopped onion, and a sprinkling of coriander.

Makes about 1$^1/_2$ quarts; 4 first-course servings with extra for freezing, or 4 main-course servings.

DOWN-HOME SPLIT-PEA SOUP

When I made this on national TV, the recipe requests poured in.

1 pound dried split green peas
1 1/2 quarts chicken stock
2 large smoked ham hocks
2 cups milk
1 large onion, chopped
1 large potato, peeled and diced
2 bay leaves
3 dashes of hot pepper sauce
1 to 2 tablespoons fresh dill
Freshly ground pepper to taste

Rinse the split peas and combine them with all the other ingredients in a large pot. Bring to a boil, then reduce heat and bring the liquid to a simmer. Cover and cook 1 1/2 hours, stirring occasionally.

Remove the cover and cook an additional hour. Remove the ham hocks and trim the meat by discarding fat and bone. Return the meat to the pot and cook an additional hour. *Makes approximately 2 quarts.*

"A TOUCH OF SPRING" SOUP

This light spring soup is best at room temperature, a perfect first course.

1 bunch watercress (about 3 cups)
1 medium zucchini
1 medium onion
2 cloves garlic
2 tablespoons unsalted butter
2 cups chicken stock
1/4 teaspoon white pepper
1 teaspoon curry powder
1 teaspoon prepared horseradish
Salt, if desired

Wash the watercress and slice the zucchini. In a large saucepan, sweat the onion and garlic in the butter, and add the chicken stock and seasonings. Add the watercress and zucchini and cook about 12 minutes, or until tender. Purée in a blender or food processor. Cool in the refrigerator and serve at room temperature. *Serves 6 to 8.*

GAZPACHO

In late August, when Dad's tomato crop seems to ripen all at once, I make big batches of Gazpacho, a zesty cold Spanish vegetable soup, and serve it with sandwiches.

1 1/2 cups chicken stock
1 1/2 cups V-8 juice
5 to 6 ripe tomatoes, peeled, seeded, and cored
1 cucumber, peeled and seeded
1 medium onion, grated
1 medium green bell pepper, cored, seeded, and
    quartered
2 sprigs basil
1 clove garlic, peeled
1/4 teaspoon dried dill weed
1/4 teaspoon cumin
Dash of hot pepper sauce
1 tablespoon red-wine vinegar
1 tablespoon fresh lemon juice
Salt, if desired
Freshly ground pepper to taste

GARNISHES:
    2 tomatoes, peeled, seeded, and cored
    1 bunch scallions
    6 sprigs basil
    1 cup croutons
    Sour cream

110

Place the stock and V-8 juice in a large mixing bowl. Using the steel blade of a food processor, purée all the other soup ingredients, starting with the tomatoes. Process in 2 batches, if necessary. Pour the mixture into the bowl with the stock and juice. Taste and add pepper and salt if necessary. Refrigerate at least several hours before serving, but overnight is best.

To prepare the vegetable garnishes, chop the tomatoes coarsely, and clean and slice the scallions crosswise. Place the vegetables in separate bowls and serve the soup with croutons, a dollop of sour cream, and a sprig of fresh basil. *Serves 4 to 6.*

WINTER NIGHT SUPPER

I came up with this goulash while spending some time ice fishing in the frigid Midwestern temperatures on Lake Minnetonka, in Minnesota. It warmed us wonderfully. Serve over noodles, with bread on the side.

ANYWHERE, U.S.A. GOULASH

2 medium onions, chopped
1 clove garlic, minced
3 tablespoons unsalted butter
1 pound veal for stewing, cut into 1-inch cubes
1 pound lean pork, cut into 1-inch cubes
One 28-ounce can Italian plum tomatoes, with juice
$1/2$ teaspoon marjoram
$2 1/2$ teaspoons sweet paprika
$1 1/2$ teaspoons caraway seeds
1 bay leaf
Freshly ground pepper to taste
Salt, if desired
$1 1/2$ pounds sauerkraut, rinsed and squeezed dry
1 pound wide egg noodles
$1 1/2$ cups sour cream

In a large skillet, sauté the onions and garlic in the butter. Add the meat and brown. Lower the heat and add the tomatoes, breaking them apart in the skillet with a wooden spoon. Add the seasonings and the sauerkraut, cover, and simmer about 1 hour.

Boil the noodles when the goulash is almost ready. Immediately before serving, stir the sour cream into the goulash and check the seasoning. *Serves 6.*

SUMMER NIGHT SUPPER

One rainy day on Cape Cod, a phone call brought me news of unexpected dinner guests. I jumped on my bicycle and pedaled down to the local fish market. Here is what I made with all the wonderful "fruits of the sea," as the Italians say. It is an adaptation of the famous San Francisco cioppino, and it will bring the smell of salt air to your table, even if you are not on Cape Cod.

CAPE COD FISH STEW

Serve with white rice or linguine.

1 ½ pounds assorted fish, such as bay scallops, scrod, monkfish, and shrimp
12 cherrystone clams
12 mussels
3 large crabs
3 cloves of garlic, peeled but not sliced
3 onions, chopped
1 medium carrot, chopped
3 tablespoons olive oil
4 cups water

One 28-ounce can Italian plum tomatoes, slightly
    crushed, with juice
1 cup dry white wine
1 teaspoon capers
$1/2$ teaspoon dried thyme
$1/2$ teaspoon oregano
18 black olives, oil-cured if possible
Freshly ground pepper to taste
Salt, if desired
1 tablespoon chopped Italian parsley

Wash all the fish, peel and devein the shrimp, and scrub
the clams, mussels, and crabs.

In a large stockpot, sauté the garlic, onions, and carrot
in the olive oil until the onions are soft. Discard the garlic.
Add the water, bring to a boil, then reduce to a simmer.

Remove 1 cup of the liquid and pour it into another
large pan. Add the scrubbed clams, mussels, and crabs to this
pan. Cook over a medium-high heat for about 5 to 10 minutes, until the clams and mussels open.

Meanwhile, to the original pot add the tomatoes and
their juice, the wine, capers, thyme, oregano, olives, pepper,
and salt if desired. Cover and simmer about 20 minutes.

Remove the shellfish from the second saucepan and
strain their juices through a cheesecloth. Discard any mussels
and clams that do not open. Crack open the crabs and pick
out the meat. Add the strained juice and the uncooked fish
to the main pot and cook, covered, for another 20 minutes.
Add the clams, mussels, and crabs and cook 8 minutes longer,
uncovered.

Remove all fish to a serving platter. Raise the heat, mix
in the parsley, and reduce the sauce by approximately half
its volume. Return the seafood to the pan and heat through.
Serves 6.

VI.
Sit-Down Dinners

BUSINESS DINNER

Crabmeat-Stuffed Mushrooms
Steamed Asparagus
Tenderloin of Beef with Peppercorn Sauce
Cheesecake

❖

FAMILY GATHERING

Corned Beef
Boiled Vegetables
Aunt Ida's Apple Dessert

❖

SOCIAL DINNER

More Than a Spinach Salad
Veal Shanks with Rice (Osso Buco)
Banana-Blueberry Split Cake

❖

James Thurber once said, "Looks can be deceiving, it's eating that's believing . . ." and that is just what your guests will be saying to themselves when they come to dine at your home. Whether the occasion be business, social, or a family get-together, your food is the integral part of these gatherings; it is the centerpiece.

A perfect marriage between wine and food is the key to a great evening. When you are entertaining dinner guests, highlight the event with carefully selected wines.

Here are a few easy wine tips to help you plan a dinner party. If you plan a cocktail hour before dinner and have gone to the trouble to select good wines, do not serve hard liquor. Instead, offer champagne, or an aperitif. Serve wines to enhance food; never overwhelm it. Nor should a wine be overshadowed by the food it accompanies.

Light, dry white wines and dry sparkling white wines are perfect companions for subtle foods from the sea. Hors d'oeuvres take kindly to dry to medium-dry white wines or rosé wines. Red wines rich in bouquet, but not too full-bodied, pair handsomely with simple meats and poultry, while full-bodied reds complement heavier dishes, such as sauced pasta, stews, and game. Use the wine you plan to drink with dinner as an ingredient in preparing the foods. Never cook with a wine you would not drink. During cooking, the alcohol in wine evaporates, leaving only flavor and aroma.

A rule of thumb for buying wine is approximately 12 ounces of wine ($^1/_2$ bottle) per person for a two- or three-course meal. A glass should be filled no more than two-thirds full. If you are serving two wines, estimate 6 ounces of each wine per person. When serving more than one wine, follow these simple rules: light wine before a heavy one; dry before sweet; white before red; younger before older; and lesser quality before better quality. Since lighter food courses usually precede heavier ones and dessert is always last, it is easy to follow these rules. For the weight-conscious, remember, red or white wine contains only about 100 calories per 4-ounce glass, in contrast to 160 calories for a 4-ounce martini.

White wines should be chilled to 45° F., light reds to about 60° F.; burgundies and other rich reds should be served at room temperature and will benefit from being opened and allowed to breathe an hour or two before serving.

Champagne and sparkling wines under great pressure present a danger when opened carelessly. Don't pop the cork. Besides letting all that good "bubbly" and effervescence escape, you can injure someone or yourself if you are hit with the cork.

After removing the wire basket from the cork, always point the bottle away from you and other people. Wrap a cloth napkin around the cork. Grasp the cork and turn the bottle gently—yes, the bottle. When the cork is loosened, let the gas escape gradually and keep the good stuff from escaping and keep everyone's eyes intact.

❖

Serve aperitifs in any attractive glass of your choice—perhaps those special long-stemmed glasses you put away in the back of your closet. For champagne, use long narrow glasses, the new tulip shape. Avoid the traditional wide saucer-type glasses that were popular some years ago; they cause the bubbles to escape too rapidly. But don't throw those glasses out if you have a full set in your cupboard, they make elegant serving dishes for desserts and first courses. Be sure to use long-stemmed glasses for white wines so that the hands do not touch the chilled wine in the glass bowl. Rather than deal with the rather complicated European system of different glasses for burgundies and bordeaux, I use a 14-ounce balloon glass for all red wine. (They also are wonderful for mixed drinks and desserts.) Pour red wine only up to the half-way mark or less.

Remember, these are only wine suggestions. If you or your guests prefer to drink a wine contrary to popular practice, then by all means do so and enjoy it!

Whatever you are serving for a sit-down dinner, remember that coffee is a course and you must prepare for it. Most of us remember a dinner where the food was great, the conversation and the wine flowed freely, but the evening was brought to an abrupt end by the appearance of bad or mediocre coffee.

The first and most important rule to remember is to make the coffee fresh when you are ready to serve it. Do not make it early in the evening in an effort to save work time during the party. The coffee will be old and will taste old. And never reboil coffee.

For a great cup of coffee, it is important to start with fresh cold water. The usual correct measure is 1 level tablespoon of ground coffee for each 6 ounces of water; I prefer 1 tablespoon per 8 ounces of water. Many people prefer to use bottled spring water, depending on where they live and the taste of their tap water. (A pinch of vitamin C powder will neutralize any unpleasant tap-water taste.)

Make sure the glass utensil used for brewing is thoroughly clean, so that the new coffee will not be affected by any residue from previous coffee.

The best way to make coffee is the drip method, using a filter. When brewing, add a dash of cinnamon to the grounds before adding the water and you'll taste a delicious difference in the mellowness of your coffee.

To preserve fresh coffee flavor, keep ground coffee in the refrigerator, whole coffee beans in the freezer.

THE BUSINESS DINNER

When you are giving a business dinner and the boss or a new client is coming to your house, you want to present your best side. The mood you create will be your signature. The food you serve will be your calling card. This should be an event that is very well planned.

Of course you will use your finest plates, linen, and silver. If you put flowers on the table for a centerpiece, be sure they are low enough so that the guests can see everyone. Depending on the season, vary the setting for each course: cocktails here, dinner in the dining room, dessert in some unexpected spot. In this way you can preset each area, and the plate clearing at the end can wait.

If your mate calls home and says "Guess who's coming to dinner?" you hope you will at least have a few hours to put together the perfect meal for the boss. It will be better for you if you have a few days. Eight years ago, I was the unexpected guest for Mrs. C. in Louisiana when Mr. C., owner of a large chain of supermarkets, persuaded me, much against my better judgment, to come home unannounced for dinner. When Mrs. C. opened the door, comfortable in her favorite robe—you know, the one with the torn pocket and hair-dye stains—and with rollers in her hair, she was not pleased. The menu that night was Monday-night meat loaf, the recipe for which you will not find in this book because it depends on leftovers from the weekend. Moral: *Never invite the boss home on the spur of the moment.*

FAMILY GATHERINGS

Sharing a meal with loved ones is always a happening, a fond time where memories are made. Fun with the family can be a special occasion, such as a birthday, anniversary, a holiday dinner, or even an impromptu visit by Aunt Millie.

Everyone should be included in the menu planning. When planning a meal, it is a good idea to check for any dietary limitations, food likes and dislikes. Don't choose fish if you know your brother-in-law hates fish, even though you may hate your brother-in-law. I also feel it's important to keep the group together. Don't let nephew Johnny turn on the TV or let his father watch the football game. Set the mood in your house that this is a family function, not a tailgate party. Don't let all the females gather in the kitchen and all the males gather in front of the TV.

Try not to use a family dinner with relatives as a platform to air grievances. Personal worries, school problems, discipline problems, and other negative aspects of daily life do not make a merry evening. Remember that favorite aunt you always enjoyed visiting because she made everything so special, so different. I am sure her food was delicious, but her *hospitality* was probably her secret. She thought of little treats for the children and impromptu games to add to the fun.

THE SOCIAL DINNER

Your coworkers, neighbors, or friends are coming for dinner. It needn't be as formal as a business situation, but by paying extra attention to details and to the menu, you show respect for the friendship.

People like to be entertained, not just come on in, pull up a chair, and dig in. Conversation becomes more interesting when friends are gathered around the table to share a meal together. Even for familiar friends, your choice of food to be served should reflect some thought and originality. Offer the hospitality you would welcome yourself. Your efforts will be rewarded because your friends will remember the evening. Warmth and friendliness make good food taste *excellent*.

As for the structure of the meal itself, have everything planned out ahead of time. Little jobs like fixing drinks or opening the wine can be delegated by the host. There will be a tendency for your friends to want to pitch in and volunteer or to get up to help clear. Try to keep them out of the kitchen-duty jobs.

This is a question that comes up often: If a guest brings a bottle of wine or dessert, should it become part of the evening's fare? I usually play that by ear. If the wines are already planned or the gift bottle does not go with what you're serving or there may not be enough for the group to share, save it for another time.

If the dessert is homemade cookies or candy, it can be added to your planned dessert. If it is similar to your dessert—such as a cake, mousse, et cetera—serve *yours* first, and then offer your gift for seconds.

PROPER PLACE SETTINGS

Formal

You will use several different wineglasses. A salad plate may be added to the left of the forks. The most formal dinners will have a cover plate or service plate onto which the plate with the first course or starters can be placed. Remove the cover plate before the entrée arrives. On the left side of the plate and closest to it is the main fork, next the fish or appetizer fork, then the salad fork, in the order that the courses are served. On the right side and closest to the plate is the main knife, next the fish knife, and on the outside the soup spoon. A butter knife rests on the bread plate that is positioned above the forks to the left of the dinner plate. Dessert spoons and forks may be placed above the plate between the glasses and the bread-and-butter plate, or they may be brought in with dessert. The glasses are placed on the right side above the silverware or flatware. Left to right are water glass, red-wine glass, white-wine glass. Dishes are taken away and fresh ones are served with each added course. The napkin is laid flat with a simple fold and centered on the dinner plate.

Informal

Informal table settings are recognized easily by only one or two glasses, and by the presence of both soup and dessert spoons at the same time. On the left side of the plate and closest to it is the main fork, next the salad fork. On the right side and closest to the plate is the main knife, next the coffee and dessert spoon, next the soup spoon. Glass service is on the right side above the flatware. Left to right are the water glass and wineglass. In the absence of a salad plate, the bread plate is positioned directly to the left of the salad fork. No separate fish or appetizer knife and fork is provided. The napkin may be fanfolded over the dinner plate or creatively rolled into the empty water goblet; or it can be laid flat to the left of the forks, with the bread plate above the forks.

MENU SELECTION

It's important to realize that at dinner parties when everyone is talking over food, there is probably a tendency to eat more than usual. You have gone to the trouble to make the food extra special, so be sure you have more than enough. It is better to err on the side of too much than not enough. You can always freeze leftovers for future meals, so nothing is wasted.

Foods should fit the time and mood. You and your family may not dine on lobster or filet mignon every day, but you may want to serve it for special occasions or when you want to make an impression.

You will have to disappear into the kitchen from time to time, but these trips should be short. Everything should be well thought out and orchestrated so that at serving time, it is a matter of pushing buttons, turning things on, and dressing the plates. Rotate the kitchen duties with other members of the family and arrange beforehand which course they will serve and clear. You will find that if you organize when and how the food will get to the table, the evening and the conversation will flow.

Of course, it is comforting if you have outside help for a dinner party. If you entertain often, find someone who is competent and who you can use frequently. It could be a neighbor's teenager, whom you could break in and help teach to serve and clear and keep things in order in the kitchen. You'll be amazed at how well this arrangement can work out for you, and at the same time you are teaching while you do it.

Several days before the party, look for and check the items you will be using. Is the silver polished? Are the crystal and glassware spotless? Are dinner napkins ironed? Set the table one or two days ahead. Plan menus and purchase items that can be bought in advance. Check staples, liquors, wines, and mixers. Be sure there is room in the front closet for guests' coats to hang easily, and be sure the bathroom is cleaned up, with fresh towels put out. The evening before, do absolutely everything that can be done, and when your meal is over, leave for the next day absolutely everything that can be left until tomorrow (see tips on pages 40–41).

Here are some suggested menus and recipes. Of course, you can interchange different recipes and augment them with salads or other appetizers as you see fit. You know your guests best and what they like.

❖ *BUSINESS DINNER MENU* ❖

CRABMEAT-STUFFED MUSHROOMS   TENDERLOIN OF BEEF WITH
STEAMED ASPARAGUS   PEPPERCORN SAUCE
CHEESECAKE

This meal should not cause you anxiety if you do some of the preparation ahead of time. Make the cheesecake a day or two before the dinner. Stuff the mushrooms during the afternoon and keep them in the refrigerator. Pour the milk around them just before cooking. The beef and asparagus are relatively simple to cook, leaving you time to concentrate on the Peppercorn Sauce and to put it all together.

CRABMEAT-STUFFED MUSHROOMS

12 to 18 medium-sized mushrooms
1 cup fresh crabmeat, removed from the shell and
    broken apart, or one 6 1/2-ounce can crabmeat
3 tablespoons unsalted butter
1/4 cup cracker meal
2 tablespoons mayonnaise
1/4 teaspoon white pepper
1 tablespoon dry white vermouth
1 tablespoon grated Parmesan cheese
Salt, if desired
1 to 2 cups milk
Parsley for garnish

Preheat oven to 300° F.

Remove stems from mushroom caps and discard. Wipe caps with a damp sponge or paper towel, and set aside.

Pick over the crabmeat to remove any cartilage. Melt the butter, and mix it with the crabmeat, cracker meal, mayonnaise, pepper, vermouth, grated Parmesan, and salt, if desired. Stuff each cap with spoonfuls of the mixture, mounding it high in the center. (Any leftover filling can be frozen and used another time.) Place the caps in a small baking dish or pan just large enough to accommodate them snugly, and pour in the milk, which should come to the top of the mushrooms, just below the stuffing.

Bake in the oven until tender, approximately 45 minutes. Remove to a serving dish with a slotted spoon, and decorate with parsley. *Serves 6 to 8.*

STEAMED ASPARAGUS

Tall, lean stalks cooked to perfection are simply delicious without any added sauce. Don't overcook!

3 pounds fresh asparagus
$^1/_2$ cup melted butter, if desired
Freshly ground pepper to taste
Salt, if desired

Prepare and clean the asparagus for cooking: cut or break off pale ends and wash well. Tie in a bunch with a butcher's cord or any white string. Stand the asparagus in a deep pan with $^1/_2$ cup boiling water. Cover and simmer gently.

When the asparagus are tender, about 18 to 20 minutes depending on thickness, remove them, untie, and place in a serving dish. If you wish, pour hot butter over the asparagus, add salt and pepper, and serve. *Serves 6 to 8.*

TENDERLOIN OF BEEF WITH PEPPERCORN SAUCE

This tenderloin, with its peppery, creamy sauce, is very rich and addictive.

BEEF:

3 to 4 pounds beef tenderloin, trimmed
2 tablespoons olive oil

Rub the meat with the olive oil and place it in a small roasting pan. Turn the oven on high and then immediately reduce the heat to warm, the lowest setting on your oven dial. Place the meat in the oven for 30 minutes.

Increase the oven temperature to 450° F. for 15 to 18 minutes. The meat thermometer should read 120° F. for rare, 130° F. for medium. Let the meat rest on a platter for 10 minutes. The temperature will rise 5 degrees while it rests, so that you attain 125° F. for rare meat, 135° F. for medium.

Slice the beef to desired thickness, and serve the peppercorn sauce alongside. *Serves 6 to 8.*

PEPPERCORN SAUCE:
   $1/2$ cup unsalted butter
   $3/4$ cup thinly sliced shallots
   3 cups beef stock
   3 tablespoons peppercorns, crushed
   $3/4$ cup brandy
   2 cups heavy cream
   $1/4$ teaspoon dry mustard

Melt the butter in a skillet and add the shallots. When the shallots are translucent, pour in the beef stock and add the peppercorns. On high heat, reduce the sauce by half, stirring occasionally.

Add the brandy, cream, and dry mustard, and again reduce by half, stirring occasionally. *Makes 2 to 2$1/2$ cups.*

CHEESECAKE

A light and airy cheesecake that can be made as much as two days ahead. Serve with fresh or frozen berries of your choice.

7 egg whites
1 1/2 pounds ricotta cheese
2 egg yolks
1 cup sugar
Juice of 1/2 orange
1 1/2 tablespoons vanilla
1 tablespoon anisette liqueur
1 teaspoon orange peel
1 teaspoon baking powder
Confectioner's sugar for sprinkling

Preheat oven to 350° F.

Beat the egg whites until stiff, and set aside. Mix the ricotta cheese with the egg yolks, sugar, orange juice, vanilla, anisette, orange peel, and baking powder. Fold in the egg whites.

Pour into a greased and floured 8-inch springform pan. Bake in oven for approximately 50 minutes to 1 hour. Check with a cake tester or toothpick inserted in the center of the cake. The tester should come out clean. When cooling, a little liquid may ooze out; this is normal. Sprinkle with confectioner's sugar and serve. *Serves 8 to 12.*

❖ *FAMILY GATHERING MENU* ❖

CORNED BEEF
BOILED VEGETABLES
AUNT IDA'S APPLE DESSERT

CORNED BEEF

Corned beef is beef that has been cured in a seasoned brine solution.

One 3$\frac{1}{2}$- to 4-pound corned beef brisket
1 onion studded with 4 cloves and cut in half
2 cloves garlic, peeled and crushed
2 bay leaves
1 teaspoon peppercorns
$\frac{1}{2}$ teaspoon sugar

Place the brisket in a large pan and cover with cold water. Add the onion, garlic, bay leaves, peppercorns, and sugar. Cover the pan and bring it to a boil. Reduce heat to a simmer. After 30 minutes, skim off any foam residue.

Re-cover and cook about 3$\frac{1}{2}$ hours, or until tender. Add boiling water if any has evaporated. As with most meats and poultry taken directly from the heat, let it rest 5 to 10 minutes before carving.

Slice the brisket against the grain. Lay the slices in the center of a large platter and surround it at both ends with cabbage, rutabaga, onions, and carrots, as cooked in the following recipe. I like to arrange the meat slices so they do not look picture-perfect but somewhat casual. *Serves 6 to 8.*

BOILED VEGETABLES

Although many people cook their vegetables in the same pan as the brisket, I prefer to cook them separately and use this stock later for soup. Start preparing the vegetables halfway through the cooking time of the beef, so that they are both done at the same time.

If you object to the odors from cooking cabbage; add a few celery stalks or tops to the pot.

1 medium head cabbage, cut in half
6 small potatoes, scrubbed, with skins on
1 small rutabaga, peeled
3 large carrots, peeled and cut in half
3 medium onions, peeled and cut in half
2 bay leaves
1 teaspoon caraway seeds
1 teaspoon peppercorns
Salt, if desired

Clean and prepare the vegetables and put them in a large pan. Cover with water. Add the bay leaves, caraway seeds, peppercorns, and salt if desired. Cover the pan and bring to a boil; reduce to a simmer and cook about 30 minutes.

Check the vegetables to see if they are done, and cook a few minutes longer if needed. Drain the vegetables and reserve the stock for a later use. Cut the cabbage halves into 3 pieces each. Arrange the vegetables, as suggested in the preceding recipe, on opposite ends of the serving platter around the corned beef. *Serves 6 to 8.*

AUNT IDA'S APPLE DESSERT

*My Aunt Ida likes to make this, and I have news for you:
it is outrageously simple but delectable. Serve with the very best
vanilla ice cream.*

$^1/_2$ cup unsalted butter
$^1/_2$ cup raisins
1 cup crumbled oatmeal cookies
$^1/_2$ cup flour
4 large baking apples, peeled, cored, and sliced
1 cup brown sugar
Juice of 1 lemon
$^1/_4$ teaspoon cinnamon
$^1/_4$ teaspoon freshly grated nutmeg

Preheat oven to 350° F.

Melt the butter in a skillet. Add the raisins and crumbled
cookies. Stir over low heat until all are coated with butter.
Remove from the heat and mix in the flour.

Lay half the apples in an 8-inch-round greased casserole
or soufflé dish. Sprinkle them with $^1/_2$ cup brown sugar and
half the lemon juice. Make another layer with the remaining
apples, and add the rest of the brown sugar and lemon juice.
Top off with the cookie mixture. Sprinkle the top with cinnamon and nutmeg.

Bake approximately 45 minutes. *Serves 6.*

❖ *SOCIAL DINNER MENU* ❖

MORE THAN A SPINACH SALAD
VEAL SHANKS WITH RICE (OSSO BUCO)
BANANA-BLUEBERRY SPLIT CAKE

MORE THAN A SPINACH SALAD

1 1/2 pounds crisp fresh spinach
1 red onion, thinly sliced
2 small-to-medium zucchini, sliced into thin
    matchsticks
3 hard-boiled egg whites, thinly sliced

DRESSING:
2 raw eggs
2 dashes of Worchestershire sauce
3 tablespoons grated Parmesan cheese
Juice of 1 1/2 lemons
1 teaspoon Dijon mustard
1/2 cup olive oil
1 1/2 teaspoons sugar
Freshly ground pepper to taste
Salt, if desired
6 slices bacon, cooled, drained, and crumbled

Wash the spinach thoroughly to remove all sand, drain, and dry. Place the spinach, onion, zucchini, and cooked egg whites in a large salad bowl. Chill until ready to serve.

Combine all dressing ingredients except the bacon in a blender or food processor. Add the bacon and the dressing to the salad; toss and serve. *Serves 6 to 8.*

VEAL SHANKS WITH RICE
(OSSO BUCO)

Serve this with plain white rice cooked with $1/4$ teaspoon tumeric added to the rice water.

6 large veal shanks, 3 inches thick by 4 to $4^1/2$ inches
    wide (if smaller, allow 2 per person)
$1/2$ cup flour
2 tablespoons unsalted butter
2 tablespoons olive oil
1 cup white wine
2 cups beef stock
2 cups canned Italian plum tomatoes, drained and
    slightly crushed
$1/8$ teaspoon dried sage
Freshly ground black pepper to taste
Salt, if desired
1 tablespoon grated lemon peel
$1/2$ cup chopped Italian parsley
Italian parsley sprigs for garnish

Roll the shanks in the flour. Melt the butter with the oil in a large skillet big enough to hold all shanks in one layer and brown them on all sides over medium-high heat.

Lower the heat and pour in $1/4$ cup wine and $1/4$ cup beef stock. Cover and cook at a slow simmer for 40 minutes.

Remove the shanks and defat the pan juices. Add the tomatoes to the juices in the pan with the remainder of the beef stock, the sage, pepper, and salt if desired. Combine.

Return the shanks to the pan and pour in the remainder of the wine. Cover and continue to cook for 1 3/4 to 2 hours, watching that the contents do not boil but simmer very slowly. The meat should be very tender, so use tongs to remove the shanks to a warm platter when done.

Sprinkle a little of the lemon peel on each shank. Turn up the heat, add chopped parsley, and reduce the sauce by half its volume. Place each shank on an individual serving plate and encircle it with rice. Spoon on the sauce, crisscrossing over the meat. Garnish with parsley sprigs and serve. *Serves 6.*

BANANA-BLUEBERRY SPLIT CAKE

You can make this up to two days ahead of time. It also freezes well. You can serve this with the very best vanilla ice cream.

1 1/2 cups light olive oil or vegetable oil
2 1/2 cups sugar
1 1/2 teaspoons vanilla
3 eggs
3 cups flour
1 teaspoon baking soda
3/4 teaspoon salt
1/2 cup pecans, chopped
1 cup fresh or frozen thawed blueberries
1/2 cup buttermilk
2 bananas, mashed

Preheat the oven to 325° F.

In a large bowl, mix the oil, sugar, vanilla, and eggs. Stir in the flour, baking soda, and salt, and mix well. Mix in the pecans and blueberries. Add the buttermilk and bananas and mix thoroughly.

Bake in a greased tube pan for approximately 1 1/2 hours. *Serves 8 to 10.*

VII.

Entertaining, Cocktails

COCKTAILS

❖

NONALCOHOLIC DRINKS

❖

HORS D'OEUVRES

Stuffed Snow Peas
Spiced Beef
Sweet Roasted Peppers with Sausage in Pita Bread
Stuffed Tuscan Peppers
Olive Toast Squares
Cheese Pie Squares
Chicken Tiki
Pork Tidbits
Meatballs
Easy Clam Fritters
Bagna Calda (Garlic and Anchovy Bath)

❖

COCKTAILS

If you are giving the all-American cocktail party, you will need a good mix of guests, liquid refreshments, and some nifty nibbles, known as canapés or hors d'oeuvres. Be creative and serve finger foods that are easy for guests to handle. Food at a cocktail party is important to help fortify those drinking alcoholic beverages. It is also becoming very popular to dealcoholize cocktails for the many people who do not drink alcohol. It is flattering to nondrinkers to be offered creative nonalcoholic alternatives other than a cola or ginger ale. (See nonalcoholic drink suggestions on pages 161–64.)

To me, liquid refreshments are as important as the food served when entertaining. They should be thoughtfully selected. These are some guidelines to help you take stock and suggest needed supplies for cocktail parties. Remember, a vodka drinker doesn't like to drink rye or gin, so be prepared to have a good supply of all the basics on hand. Liquor keeps well and doesn't spoil, but if you have bought too much for a big party, most stores will take back unopened bottles. The essential liquors are vodka, gin, rye, scotch, bourbon, Cognac or brandy, tequila, dry and sweet vermouth, aperitifs like Lillet or Dubonnet, and some sherry and port for after dinner.

How Much Liquor Do You Need?

When planning and buying your liquor, the most economical bottle is the liter, containing 33.8 ounces, or 22 drinks, when calculated at 1 1/2 ounces a drink. One 750-milliliter bottle of still wine (25.4 ounces) will pour 5 glasses of wine. The same size bottle of champagne or sparkling wine will yield enough for 6 flute-sized glasses.

Unless you are premixing pitchers of Bloody Marys or Screwdrivers, you should have brand-name liquors available. Pick the most popular scotch, rye, vodka, gin, and so forth.

Have fruits and all the other garnishes ready just before your guests arrive. It is awkward and unprepared to have to fetch this and grab that at the last minute.

Where to Set Up the Bar

Choose a location away from the front door, and most definitely not in the kitchen. Most people grab a drink and tend to gravitate around the bar area, creating a bottleneck.

If your guests are mixing their own drinks, check the ice, soda, water, et cetera, often. If you have someone mixing drinks, check in with him or her frequently and also make sure that your special no-alcohol mixed concoctions are being offered. Watch for guests drinking too much, too fast, too soon.

It is in your best interest as the host to avoid drinking

until the party is nearly over. Also, when you see a guest drinking too much, make him or her a drink with little or no alcohol.

Here are some traditional cocktails, followed by a few of my favorite specialties.

MANHATTAN

2 1/2 ounces rye or bourbon
1/2 ounce sweet vermouth
Dash of bitters
Lemon twist

PERFECT MANHATTAN

My experience is that the sweet/dry vermouth mixture makes this a very powerful drink. Therefore I have decreased the amount of whiskey.

1 1/2 ounces rye or bourbon
1/4 ounce dry vermouth
1/4 ounce sweet vermouth
Dash of bitters
Lemon twist

Pour the whiskey, vermouth, and bitters over ice, and stir. Strain into a 4-ounce cocktail glass. Garnish with lemon twist. This may also be served on the rocks in a short glass.

HIGHBALL

2 ounces rye, bourbon, or scotch
Thin lemon slice or twist
Soda water or ginger ale

Combine ingredients and serve in a tall glass with ice.

OLD-FASHIONED

1 lump of sugar
Dash of bitters
Twist of lemon peel
2½ ounces rye
Slice of orange

Place sugar in a short glass with a drop of water to dissolve it. Add the bitters, ice cubes, and lemon peel. Fill with rye. Stir, and decorate with the orange slice.

MINT JULEP

I mixed this at Churchill Downs on national television two days before the 1989 Derby and then had the pleasure of picking the Derby winner.

2 mint sprigs
1 teaspoon superfine sugar
2 teaspoons water
3 ounces bourbon
Splash of soda, if desired
Mint leaf for garnish

Let the mint, sugar, and water set in a glass for a few minutes until mint flavor is released from the leaves. Add the bourbon. Strain and pour into a glass with crushed ice and add a splash of soda, if desired. Garnish with a mint leaf.

BOURBON SOUR

2 ounces bourbon
1 ounce lemon juice or sour mix
$1/2$ teaspoon superfine sugar

Shake ingredients in a covered jar or a cocktail shaker, and pour into a short glass with ice.

For a Whiskey Sour, Scotch Sour, Vodka Sour, Rum Sour, or Tequila Sour, follow above recipe, replacing bourbon with the appropriate liquor.

IRISH COFFEE

This is the recipe that won Maureen O'Hara's heart.

1 teaspoon raw sugar
Freshly brewed hot coffee
1 1/2 ounces Irish whiskey
Lightly whipped cream
Optional:
Shaved chocolate for garnish

In a traditional glass Irish coffee mug, dissolve the sugar with a little hot coffee. Pour in the Irish whiskey. Fill the mug with coffee to approximately an inch of the brim, and then add whipped cream gently over the back of a spoon (so as not to mix); cream should float on top. Garnish with shaved chocolate, if desired. Serve immediately.

BLOODY MARY

Make a batch of the juice mix with or without the vodka and store in the refrigerator ahead of time to avoid laboring over each drink. Serves 4.

8 ounces vodka
16 ounces V-8 juice
Juice of $\frac{1}{2}$ lemon
1 tablespoon Worcestershire sauce
$\frac{1}{8}$ teaspoon hot red pepper sauce
Dash of celery salt
Dash of pepper
$\frac{1}{2}$ teaspoon prepared horseradish
$\frac{1}{8}$ teaspoon bitters
4 lemon wedges for garnish

Serve in a tall all-purpose wineglass.

BULLSHOT
Substitute beef bouillon for the V-8 juice in the above recipe.

GAZPACHO MARY
For a tasty summer variation substitute cold Gazpacho (page 110) for the juice mix above.

BLACK RUSSIAN

1 1/2 ounces vodka
3/4 ounce coffee liqueur

Mix ingredients over ice in short glass.

WHITE RUSSIAN

1 1/4 ounces vodka
1 1/4 ounces coffee liqueur
2 ounces half-and-half or light cream

Shake ingredients with ice.

NEGRONI

This is one of my favorites!

1 ½ ounces gin
1 ounce Campari
1 ounce sweet vermouth
Optional:
Splash of soda
Twist of orange

Serve this drink in a short glass. You may add a splash of club soda and garnish with a twist of orange.
For a Vodka Negroni, substitute vodka for the gin.

SCREWDRIVER

2 ounces vodka
Orange juice

Put 2 to 3 ice cubes in highball glass. Add the vodka, then fill glass with orange juice. Stir.

EXTRA-DRY MARTINI

2 ounces gin
Dash of dry vermouth
Lemon twist or small green olive

Stir gin and vermouth with cracked ice, and strain into cocktail glass. This may also be served on the rocks. For a less dry martini, add up to $1/2$ ounce dry vermouth.

GIBSON
If the lemon or olive is replaced with a pickled onion, it becomes a Gibson.
For an Extra-Dry Vodka Martini or Gibson, substitute vodka for the gin.

TOM COLLINS

Juice of $1/2$ lemon or Collins mix
$1/2$ teaspoon sugar, or to taste
2 ounces gin
Soda water
Orange slice

Fill a large glass with ice. Add juice or mix, sugar, and gin. Fill with soda water, and garnish with orange slice.
For a Vodka Collins, Bourbon Collins, Scotch Collins, or Rum Collins, follow the above recipe, replacing the gin with the appropriate liquor.

PIÑA COLADA

2 ounces light rum
2 ounces cream of coconut
3 ounces pineapple juice
Pineapple slice for garnish

Combine rum, cream of coconut, and juice with $\frac{1}{2}$ cup cracked ice in a blender. Garnish with pineapple.

LOVE POTION

Here is a drink I developed for a series of parties for the government of Puerto Rico. Don't serve more than two to anyone, except maybe yourself and your love when the party is over.

1 $\frac{1}{2}$ ounces papaya juice
1 $\frac{1}{2}$ ounces light rum
$\frac{1}{2}$ ounce pineapple juice
Superfine sugar or simple syrup to taste
1 teaspoon grenadine
Club soda

Mix all the ingredients except the club soda in a jar or cocktail shaker. Pour over ice and top with club soda.

FATHER'S DAY CELEBRATION PUNCH

4 cups cranberry juice, chilled
2 cups seltzer or salt-free club soda, chilled
2 cups coconut rum, chilled
Orange, lemon, and lime slices for garnish, if desired

In a large punch bowl, gently stir together the cranberry juice, seltzer, and coconut rum. Add ice, top with orange, lemon, and lime slices, if desired, and serve. *Makes 2 quarts; sixteen 1/2-cup servings.*

KIR

5 ounces white wine or champagne
1/2 ounce crème de cassis

Pour the crème de cassis into a champagne flute, then add chilled wine or champagne.

BRANDY CHAMPAGNE COCKTAILS

This is one of my favorite special drinks.

Lemon juice
Sugar
1 ounce brandy
4 ounces champagne
2 teaspoons simple syrup

Dip a champagne flute in lemon juice, then in sugar, in order to coat the rim. Add the brandy, champagne, and simple syrup.

SIMPLE SYRUP:
Simple syrup is sugar water that instantly sweetens drinks without having to dissolve, thus eliminating sugar at the bottom of your drink.

Boil ²/₃ cup sugar and ¹/₃ cup water for 5 minutes. Place in a jar and keep refrigerated until needed. It will keep a long time. When substituting for sugar, 1 spoonful equals 1 spoonful of sugar.

BELLINI

2 ounces peach juice, squeezed from fresh peaches or
    bottled concentrate
4 ounces ice-cold champagne or dry white wine
Dash of grenadine, if desired

Combine ingredients and serve straight up.

BRANDY ALEXANDER

1 ounce brandy
1 ounce crème de cacao
1 ounce heavy cream

Shake ingredients with cracked ice. Strain into cocktail
glass and serve straight up.

STINGER

This is usually an after-dinner drink.

2 ounces brandy
1 ounce white crème de menthe

Shake ingredients with crushed ice. Strain and serve
straight up.

NONALCOHOLIC DRINKS

I'd like to let you in on a secret: You can make many of the traditional mixed drinks like Bloody Marys, piña coladas, and daiquiris with *no liquor*, that's right, *no liquor*. Anything that has scotch, rye, or bourbon won't work this way, but a majority of fruit-based sweetened mixtures made with gin, vodka, or rum will taste fine without alcohol. I often serve piña coladas just as a juice and add extra soda. A Bloody Mary without liquor is a Virgin Mary; bullshots are also good without the vodka.

Another useful trick is to serve cold soups as beverages for nondrinkers. The recipe for Gazpacho (page 110) can be turned into a Gazpacho Mary, a tasty summer variation on a Virgin Mary.

APRICOT-YOGURT SHAKE

$1/2$ cup apricot nectar, chilled
$1/2$ cup vanilla yogurt
Freshly grated nutmeg for dusting

Combine apricot nectar and yogurt and shake well. Serve over ice and sprinkle with nutmeg.

A NEW HORIZON

Orange juice
1 tablespoon frozen limeade concentrate
Club soda
Cranberry juice

Fill a tall glass halfway with orange juice; add limeade and mix until it dissolves. Add ice. Fill almost to the top with club soda. Stir. Top off with cranberry juice. Do not stir, but let cranberry juice trickle through drink for visual effect.

BITTERS AND SODA

Although bitters contain a small amount of alcohol, I use it as a flavoring for this refreshing drink.

Club soda
Bitters
Lemon or orange twist

Add club soda to a tall glass filled with ice. Add a dash or two of bitters and stir. Serve with a twist.

SMOOTH SAILING

Pear nectar
Cranberry juice
1 tablespoon frozen lemonade concentrate

Fill a tall glass halfway with pear nectar, then fill up to one-quarter from top with cranberry juice. Add lemonade and stir well. Add ice and serve.

GINGER ALE AND TEA

3 ounces strong tea, chilled
3 ounces ginger ale
2 ounces orange juice
1 lemon wedge

Add tea, ginger ale, and orange juice to a tall glass filled with ice. Stir. Squeeze in and add lemon wedge.

SAN FRANCISCO PUNCH

One 10-ounce package frozen strawberries, or 1 pint
   fresh strawberries
4 quarts seltzer or salt-free club soda
One 6-ounce can frozen lemonade
One 6-ounce can frozen grapefruit juice
3 dashes of bitters

Purée strawberries in a blender. Mix purée with the seltzer, lemonade, grapefruit juice, and bitters in a large punch
bowl. Add ice cubes. *Makes twelve 7-ounce servings.*

HORS D'OEUVRES

Generally, when planning for pass-arounds at a cocktail party, I usually figure about eight pieces per person. Keep in mind that guests may be trying to keep to a diet of some sort and, if convenient, offer crudités of fresh vegetables with a dip.

If your cocktail party is preceding a dinner, the food you serve during cocktails should be light. You don't want your guests to fill up during the cocktail hour and have no room for dinner. If your cocktail party is the entire event for the evening, the opposite is true; you want to serve solid, rib-sticking hors d'oeuvres.

The following recipes are finger foods I serve at cocktail-party events. Be sure to provide plenty of small plain napkins.

STUFFED SNOW PEAS

This recipe can easily be cut in half for smaller parties.

48 snow peas
One 8-ounce package cream cheese
2 tablespoons Dijon mustard
1 medium clove garlic, crushed
1 teaspoon finely minced onion
2 tablespoons minced fresh parsley

Remove the stems and strings from the snow peas. Blanch them less than 30 seconds; rinse in cold water and pat dry. Slit open the snow peas, but avoid cutting them to the extreme ends.

In a bowl, combine the cream cheese, mustard, garlic, onion, and parsley. Spoon the filling into a small, strong plastic bag, and cut off one corner, so you can use it as a throw-away pastry bag. Squeeze the filling into the pea pods. You can also do this with a butter knife. This cream-cheese mixture can also be used as a spread on slices of other vegetables. *Makes 48 hors d'oeuvres.*

SPICED BEEF

3/4 pound lean beef
1-inch piece of fresh ginger
1/3 cup water
4 tablespoons soy sauce
1/4 cup sherry
1 teaspoon sugar

Slice the beef into thin pieces. Peel the ginger and thinly slice it.

In a saucepan, combine the ginger with the water, soy sauce, sherry, and sugar. Bring to a boil, reduce heat, and let simmer for approximately 15 minutes, for ginger to flavor stock.

Add the beef to the saucepan and continue to simmer until the liquid evaporates, approximately 15 minutes. Serve the beef on small rounds of French bread or cocktail rye bread. *Makes approximately 24 to 30 pieces.*

SWEET ROASTED PEPPERS WITH SAUSAGE IN PITA BREAD

1 1/2 pounds sweet Italian sausages
Three 7 1/4-ounce jars of sweet roasted peppers
2 tablespoons unsalted butter
Pinch of oregano
Pinch of parsley
Freshly ground pepper to taste
12 mini pita breads, cut in half

Parboil the sausages for about 5 minutes. Drain the peppers and finely chop them in the food processor.

Melt the butter in a skillet and add the chopped peppers. Finely chop the sausages in the food processor, and mix them with the peppers in the pan. Add the oregano, parsley, and pepper and cook approximately 12 to 15 minutes.

Serve in small pita bread pockets, or purée further and use as a spread on small rounds of French bread or on endive leaves. *Makes approximately 24 hors d'oeuvres.*

STUFFED TUSCAN PEPPERS

One 9-ounce jar Tuscan peppers
2 anchovy fillets, drained, washed, and patted dry
2 ounces cream cheese
Dash of cayenne pepper

Drain the peppers and slit them horizontally. In a bowl, mix the anchovies with the cream cheese and cayenne pepper. Using a pastry bag or a knife, fill each pepper. *Makes approximately 18 hors d'oeuvres.*

OLIVE TOAST SQUARES

$1/2$ cup pitted black olives, chopped
9 slices thinly sliced white bread
$1 1/2$ tablespoons olive oil
$3/4$ teaspoon dried thyme

Cut the olives into thin slices. Cut the crusts off the bread, and brush the bread with olive oil. Sprinkle the thyme onto the bread and cut into $1 1/2$-inch squares. Lightly toast the bread squares under the broiler.

Remove from the broiler. Spread the olives over the toast squares, and serve immediately. *Makes about 3 dozen squares.*

CHEESE PIE SQUARES

1 medium onion, diced
1 green bell pepper, diced
$^1/_2$ teaspoon paprika
1 pound Jarlsberg cheese, shredded
6 eggs, beaten
1 pimento, cut in thin strips

Preheat the oven to 350°F.

Layer onion and green pepper in a well-buttered 8-inch-square baking pan. Sprinkle the paprika on the vegetables, and top with the cheese. Pour the beaten eggs over all. Bake in the oven for approximately 35 minutes, or until the eggs are set.

When cool, cut into 1 $^1/_2$-inch squares. Turn each square upside down, garnish with the pimento strips, and serve. This may be baked ahead and reheated, or served at room temperature. *Makes about 24 squares.*

CHICKEN TIKI

2 pounds boned chicken
$1/4$ cup soy sauce
2 cloves garlic, crushed
$1/2$ cup olive oil
1 tablespoon ground ginger
$1/2$ cup dark rum
Juice of $1/2$ orange
1 tablespoon honey
1 cup pineapple chunks

Cut the chicken into bite-size pieces. Combine all the other ingredients except the pineapple chunks, and marinate the chicken in the mixture overnight in a covered bowl in the refrigerator.

When you are ready to cook, place a piece of pineapple and a chicken piece on a regular-size toothpick. Baste once before putting in the broiler. Broil, not too close to the heat (one shelf away) 15 to 20 minutes. *Makes approximately 36 hors d'oeuvres.*

PORK TIDBITS

2 pounds pork loin
$\frac{1}{2}$ cup unsalted butter
Juice of 1 lemon
4 tablespoons apricot preserves
$\frac{1}{2}$ cup soy sauce
$\frac{1}{3}$ cup A-1 steak sauce
2 dashes of hot pepper sauce
$\frac{1}{2}$ cup gold rum

Cut the pork loin into 2-by-1$\frac{1}{2}$-inch strips. Melt butter in a pan, and mix in the lemon juice, apricot preserves, soy sauce, A-1 sauce, and hot pepper sauce. Place the pork and rum in a bowl and pour the heated marinade over the meat.

Marinate in the refrigerator for several hours. When ready to serve, drain the meat strips and broil them for about 6 minutes. Serve with toothpicks. *Makes approximately 48 strips.*

MEATBALLS

1 pound ground beef
1 pound ground pork
1 large onion, finely minced
1 clove garlic, finely minced
3 tablespoons water
2 eggs, beaten
1 1/2 cups bread crumbs
3 tablespoons soy sauce
4 tablespoons dark rum
2 tablespoons ground ginger
Freshly ground pepper to taste
Salt, if desired
Flour to coat
3/4 cup olive oil for frying
Sesame stick snacks

Place the ground meats in a large bowl. Sweat the onion and garlic in 3 tablespoons water in a covered pan. When the onion is soft, mix into the meat with the beaten eggs, bread crumbs, soy sauce, rum, ginger, pepper, and salt if desired. Form the mixture into small bite-size 1-inch meatballs. Roll the meatballs in flour, fry about 6 minutes, and drain on paper towels. Push a sesame stick into each meatball for an edible holder. *Makes approximately 36 meatballs.*

EASY CLAM FRITTERS

These clam fritters make great cocktail-party food. You can make them ahead and reheat at party time.

1½ cups sifted all-purpose flour
3½ teaspoons baking powder
Two 10½-ounce cans white clam sauce
1 egg
1 teaspoon powdered ginger
½ teaspoon freshly grated nutmeg
½ teaspoon cayenne pepper
1½ tablespoons sesame seeds
1 tablespoon chopped fresh parsley
Freshly ground pepper to taste
Salt, if desired
Vegetable oil for frying

Sift together the flour and baking powder. Drain the liquid from the clam sauce and reserve. Mix the clams with the flour and baking powder. Beat the egg, and add it to the flour mixture with the ginger, nutmeg, cayenne pepper, sesame seeds, parsley, pepper, salt if desired, and 1 cup of the reserved clam liquid.

Heat the oil to 375°F. Using two teaspoons, plunge one into the batter and use the other spoon to push the batter into the hot oil. The fritters will puff up. Fry until fritters turn golden, approximately 2 minutes, and turn over. Cook 1½ to 2 minutes more.

Remove the fritters to paper towels to absorb the extra oil. Serve hot. Can be refrigerated for later use. To reheat, place the fritters in 350°F. oven for approximately 15 to 20 minutes, or in average microwave for 2½ to 3 minutes on power 4. *Makes about 3 to 4 dozen fritters, depending on size.*

BAGNA CALDA
(Garlic and Anchovy Bath)

½ pound (1 cup) unsalted butter
¾ cup extra-virgin olive oil
4 cloves garlic, finely chopped
6 anchovy fillets, rinsed
Freshly ground pepper to taste

Prepare fresh vegetables of your choice for dipping. For example, cut celery into sticks, cucumbers and tomatoes into wedges, cauliflower into florets, zucchini into slices, peppers into quarters, et cetera.

Heat the butter and oil together, add the garlic, and gently cook for a few minutes. Add the anchovies and stir until they dissolve. Maintain heat at low temperature in a chafing dish.

Provide long wooden sticks for guests to spear the vegetables and immerse them in the hot dip for a few seconds. *Makes enough to coat 4 to 5 dozen pieces of vegetables.*

VIII.
Entertaining, Buffets

Eggplant Relish
Eggplant, Szechuan Style

❖

La Dolce Vita: Chicken and Sausage Stew
Chicken Salad Julie

❖

Kentucky Glazed Ham
Veal Marengo
Brown Rice
Stuffed Lamb à la Parma

❖

Mélange of Vegetables
Kim Chee Salad (Pickled Vegetables)

❖

Poached Pears Dubonnet

❖

The most important consideration when planning a buffet is where and how people will dine. Will they stand or sit? How will they balance food and drink and shake hands? How will they be able to cut their food? Will anything drip? Where will dirty dishes go when they are finished?

Obviously, if guests are seated and have a table to rest their plate on, then your selection of food will be different, since a knife can be used easily. If they are standing, then you must consider dishes like casseroles, finger foods, and sandwiches. For buffets, I always plan food that is not heavily sauced, to avoid dripping. And be observant to take guests' dishes from them when they are finished; otherwise plates and silverware will end up on furniture and in other unusual places.

At certain times of the year, especially at Christmas and New Year's, many hosts extend invitations to holiday open-house parties. Friends, relatives, and neighbors make the rounds, enjoying holiday cheer and a variety of foods. When they arrive at your house, make sure the food you have set out on the buffet table doesn't look tired or bedraggled from a few hours on the front line. Some foods, like shrimp, hot pastas, or cream sauces that might separate, are not good choices for the buffet table. Nor are prissy, overly fussy dishes like salmon in pastry. For safety reasons do not serve raw fish unless it is well iced and do not let pâtés made of organ meats sit out for long periods of time.

For big parties, I like large carve-your-own roasts, ham, roast beef, turkey, and complementary salads, like a huge Caesar salad or a curried potato salad. Potato frittatas hold up well, as do stews and chilis. I always put out a choice of breads—dark pumpernickel, rye, French, and Italian—as well as dressings like horseradish, sour cream, mustard, and mayonnaise that will enable my guests to make sandwiches at will. When the food is plentiful and hearty, arriving guests can join right in. At a holiday party, when guests come at different times, place homemade desserts with the gifts of candy and cookies brought by your guests at one end of the table, along with large pots of coffee and tea.

It is important to set up the buffet table so the flow of guests will be able to move around the table, rather than having to wait in line to serve themselves. There will be food on the table that certain guests will pass up and others will want. And just as important, if not the most important, is the placement of your bar. Cocktail dips and cheeses do not belong on the buffet food table, because they cause unnecessary traffic congestion.

If you have a selection of hot dishes, it is best to put them in small or medium-sized chafing dishes and refill when needed. Food looks more appetizing in small batches. Keep an extra supply of alcohol or Sterno for fuel. If the food needs to be in a chafing dish for hours, stir it gently once in a while to avoid scorched spots. At nonholiday parties, once most guests have eaten, remove the hot food in order to set up the desserts. If a guest or two is really late, it makes better sense to fix them a plate to heat in the microwave than to keep the chafing dishes filled with tired-looking food.

EGGPLANT RELISH

This is a useful dish for entertaining because it can be made ahead and served at room temperature. It is also wonderful puréed and used as a canapé to be spread on endive or French-bread rounds.

2 cups diced celery
$\frac{1}{2}$ cup olive oil
1 large or 2 medium eggplants, peeled and diced
    (about 6 cups)
1 onion, chopped
2 tablespoons tomato paste
$\frac{3}{4}$ cup water
$\frac{1}{3}$ cup red-wine vinegar
1 tablespoon sugar
$\frac{1}{2}$ cup chopped pitted green olives
1 tablespoon capers
1 tablespoon chopped fresh parsley

Sauté the celery in the olive oil until soft and translucent, about 6 minutes. Remove the celery and set aside. Sauté the diced eggplant in the same pan until soft; remove from the pan and drain on paper towels to remove excess oil.

Sauté the onion in the same pan until soft. Mix the tomato paste with the water, add the mixture to the pan with the vinegar and sugar, and simmer 15 minutes. Add the eggplant and celery, and the olives, capers, and parsley. Cook an additional 10 minutes. Serve warm or cold. *Makes 24 small portions.*

EGGPLANT, SZECHUAN STYLE

This is a spicier eggplant dish that is also perfect for a buffet, since it can be made ahead and served hot or at room temperature. Serve with white rice.

SAUCE:
$1/2$ cup chicken stock
3 tablespoons soy sauce
2 tablespoons Oriental chili bean sauce
2 tablespoons sherry
4 tablespoons sugar

2 eggplants (approximately 3 pounds total weight)
Up to $1/2$ cup vegetable oil
2 cloves garlic, slivered
2 tablespoons finely chopped fresh ginger
2 scallions, thinly sliced
2 tablespoons distilled white vinegar
2 tablespoons sesame oil

Combine the sauce ingredients in a bowl, mixing well, and set aside.

Cut unpeeled eggplant into thin strips approximately 2 inches long by $1/2$ inch wide. Heat a wok or skillet with the vegetable oil. Add the eggplant and stir-fry, turning the pieces until cooked, about 4 to 6 minutes. Add extra vegetable oil if needed. Remove the eggplant to paper towels.

Reheat the wok with 1 tablespoon vegetable oil and add the garlic, ginger, and scallions. Stir-fry for approximately 1 minute. Stir in the sauce ingredients. Add the cooked eggplant, and stir until the eggplant is covered with sauce. Add the vinegar and sesame oil to the eggplant and stir. This whole process is very quick, about 1 minute. Serve hot or at room temperature. *Serves 12 to 16.*

LA DOLCE VITA
Chicken and Sausage Stew

One 3-pound chicken, deboned and cut into small
    pieces and cleaned (remove skin, if desired)
2 pounds sweet Italian sausage, sliced into ¹/₄-inch
    pieces
8 to 10 small whole potatoes with skins on
1 clove garlic
1 large onion, thinly sliced
2 large green bell peppers, cut into strips
One 16-ounce can Italian plum tomatoes, with juice
¹/₂ teaspoon oregano
Freshly ground pepper to taste
Salt, if desired

Preheat oven to 350°F.
Combine all the ingredients in a large Dutch oven or other casserole and cook in oven, covered, for 1 hour. Remove cover, increase temperature to 400°F., and cook an additional 15 minutes. *Serves 8 to 10.*

CHICKEN SALAD JULIE

This may be made a day ahead of time and refrigerated.

3 cooked boneless chicken breasts
8 ounces mozzarella
2 ounces pimento, chopped
$^1/_2$ cup sliced pitted black olives (2$^1/_4$-ounce can)
$^1/_2$ cup mayonnaise, or more to taste
1 teaspoon dried savory
Freshly ground pepper to taste

Using the steel knife of the food processor, chop the chicken by pulsing on and off. Transfer the chicken to a large bowl. Using the shredding blade, shred the mozzarella and empty it into the bowl with the chicken.

Add the pimento, olives, mayonnaise, savory, and pepper and mix well.

Serve on a platter garnished with watercress, or pack into miniature pita pockets for easy eating. *Serves 8 to 10.*

KENTUCKY GLAZED HAM

This addition to a buffet table not only looks appetizing, its taste will create a sensation.

One 12- to 14-pound ham of your choice
3/4 cup bourbon
2 cups firmly packed dark brown sugar
1/8 teaspoon ground coriander
1 tablespoon dry mustard
1 tablespoon orange marmalade
Optional:
Cloves for decoration

Bake ham as directed by packer. About 30 minutes before ham is done, remove it from oven.

If your ham has a rind, when it is cool enough to handle, cut away the rind and trim the fat to about 1/2 inch thick. Score by cutting deeply in a crisscross pattern.

Increase the oven temperature to 450°F. With a pastry brush, paint the ham all over with bourbon. Then combine the remaining bourbon with the brown sugar, coriander, mustard, and orange marmalade and pat the mixture firmly around the ham. Stud with cloves, if desired. Return ham to oven for 30 minutes more. Ham will have an appetizing and beautiful glaze. *Serves approximately 50.*

VEAL MARENGO

It is said that this was one of Napoleon's favorite dishes. It is perfect for a buffet-type party because it can be made up to two days ahead of time. Serve with the Brown Rice recipe that follows.

4 1/2 pounds stewing veal, cut into 1-inch pieces
1/2 cup flour
2 cloves garlic, peeled and crushed
2 large onions, sliced
1/2 cup olive oil
2 cups dry white wine
One 2-pound 3-ounce can Italian plum tomatoes,
   with juice
2 green bell peppers, chopped
3/4 teaspoon dried thyme
3/4 teaspoon dried tarragon
1 bay leaf
Freshly ground pepper to taste
Salt, if desired
3/4 pound sliced mushrooms
1 tablespoon brown sugar
1/2 cup water, if needed
1/2 cup chopped fresh parsley

Preheat the oven to 350°F.
Coat the veal with the flour. Sauté the garlic and onions in a skillet with a little oil until soft. Brown the veal in 3 to

4 tablespoons oil in the same skillet. You will need to cook the veal in several batches. Use extra oil, if needed.

When the veal pieces are browned, remove them to a large oven casserole, and deglaze the pan with the wine.

Chop the tomatoes and bell peppers, and add them to the casserole with the tomato juice. Add thyme, tarragon, bay leaf, pepper, and salt if desired.

Cover and cook in the preheated oven for 1 hour. Reduce the temperature to 325°F. and cook an additional 30 minutes. Stir.

Add the mushrooms. Stir the brown sugar into the mixture in the casserole and add ½ cup water, if desired, for juiciness. Continue cooking for approximately 30 minutes longer.

Sprinkle with parsley. Serve over brown rice (following recipe) or noodles. *Serves 10 to 12.*

BROWN RICE

I recommend this recipe for a buffet table because the butter helps the rice stay moist for a long time.

8 cups beef stock
½ cup unsalted butter
3 cups brown rice

Put the stock and butter in a saucepan and bring to a boil. Stir in the rice. Cover, lower the heat, and simmer for approximately 40 minutes. Remove to a chafing dish. *Serves 10 to 12.*

STUFFED LAMB À LA PARMA

1 boned leg of lamb (about 4 to 4½ pounds),
   butterflied
3 tablespoons olive oil
4 to 6 ounces spinach
1 onion, chopped
1 tablespoon unsalted butter
¼ pound prosciutto, chopped
5 tablespoons bread crumbs
Pinch of rosemary
¼ teaspoon freshly grated nutmeg
Freshly ground pepper to taste
½ cup red wine
3 tablespoons Parmesan cheese

Preheat the oven to 350°F.

Pound the lamb to flatten it as evenly as possible into a rectangular piece. Brush the top with 1 tablespoon oil.

Steam the spinach, drain well, and finely chop. Sauté the onion in the butter until soft; add the spinach, the remaining 2 tablespoons oil, the prosciutto, bread crumbs, rosemary, nutmeg, and pepper. Cook for 3 to 4 minutes. Add the wine and reduce over medium heat until the liquid is absorbed.

Arrange the filling over the entire surface of the lamb. Sprinkle the grated cheese over the filling. Carefully roll the meat in jelly-roll fashion and tie it in several places.

Cook in the oven approximately 1¼ to 1¾ hours for rare, or longer to desired doneness. *Serves approximately 12 to 14; one 3-ounce slice each.*

MÉLANGE OF VEGETABLES

This is a perfect dish because it looks appetizing on the buffet and it is in bite-size pieces. It can also be doubled easily.

3 cloves garlic, peeled but whole
$^{1}/_{2}$ cup Italian olive oil
4 medium red potatoes, skins on, cut into 1-inch
    pieces
4 zucchini, sliced lengthwise, then crosswise in
    $^{1}/_{2}$-inch slices
4 ripe tomatoes, cut into pieces
1 $^{1}/_{2}$ cups fresh snow peas
1 teaspoon dried basil
Freshly ground pepper to taste
About 1 teaspoon hot pepper sauce
Salt, if desired

Brown the garlic cloves in the oil in a large skillet. Remove the garlic and discard. Add the potatoes, cover the pan, and cook 5 minutes. Add the zucchini, tomatoes, snow peas, basil, pepper, hot pepper sauce, and salt if desired. Continue to cook, covered, about 4 minutes more. Serve in a chafing dish or at room temperature. *Serves 8 to 10.*

KIM CHEE SALAD
(Pickled Vegetables)

1 whole Chinese cabbage (bok choy)
2 Chinese turnips, or 2 cucumbers
3 1/2 cups water
3 cloves garlic, crushed
1 tablespoon sugar
1/8 teaspoon coriander
1/2 cup distilled white vinegar
4 tablespoons sesame oil
6 scallions, finely cut
1 teaspoon dried hot red pepper flakes, crushed

Separate the leaves from the cabbage and wash. Cut them into squares, approximately 1 1/2 to 2 inches. Peel the turnips or cucumbers; cut in half and thinly slice. Place the vegetables in a large covered ceramic or stainless-steel bowl.

Mix all the remaining ingredients and bring to a boil in any nonaluminum pan. Remove from the heat.

Pour the pickling ingredients over the vegetables. Refrigerate at least 24 hours. This can be made a few days in advance. *Serves 10 to 12 as a side dish.*

POACHED PEARS DUBONNET

12 ripe Bosc pears, peeled, stems intact
About 3 cups water
2 1/4 cups red Dubonnet or similar aperitif wine
2 tablespoons freshly squeezed lemon juice
3/4 cup light brown sugar
1 tablespoon grated orange rind
Juice of 1 orange
1/2 teaspoon vanilla
2 ounces pine nuts (pignoli)
1 cup heavy cream, whipped

In a pan large enough to accommodate all the pears sideways in one layer, mix the water, Dubonnet, lemon juice, brown sugar, orange rind, orange juice, and vanilla. Simmer very slowly, approximately 12 to 18 minutes, until the pears are tender but not mushy. If the liquid does not completely cover the pears, roll them over halfway through the cooking process.

Remove the pears and place them in an elegant serving dish. Add the pine nuts to remaining liquid and reduce to a delicious syrupy consistency, yielding about 1 1/2 cups.

Pour the syrup over the pears, and serve with a dollop of whipped cream. *Serves 12.*

IX.

More Entertaining, Something Different

BARBECUES

Barbecue Sauce
Barbecue Marinade
Fish Kebabs
Steamed Fish in Foil
Grilled Lamb Dinner
Sliced Tomatoes with Mozzarella and Basil
Just a Good Salad

❖

PICNICS IN THE SNOW

Mulled Wine
Fruit Salad
Poppy Seed Dressing

❖

PICNICS BY THE FIRE

Choucroute Garni (Sauerkraut with Meat)
Penne with Westphalian Ham
Vegetables, Tempura Style
Sweet-and-Sour Sauce

❖

ROMANTIC SUPPERS

Coconut Honeymoon Shrimp
Chicken in Champagne Ginger Sauce
Filet Mignon with Marsala Sauce

❖

THEME PARTIES

Kentucky Derby Grits Casserole
Cheese Fondue
Jambalaya
Pork Lo Mein

❖

BARBECUES

Outdoor cooking has become a way of life for some more than others because of geography. In climates that are warm year-round, outdoor barbecue equipment is an extension of the kitchen. Grills and accessories have been improved and refined to provide you with the capability to cook almost any food outdoors.

Planning is important. Collect your tools, condiments, and aluminum foil before you start. Keep good sanitation procedures when you cook outdoors. Foods to be cooked should be brought out at the last minute. Platters and utensils that come in contact with raw meats, poultry, or fish should be washed before being used again to serve the cooked food.

Choose a good location for setting up your barbecue. Set it up in an open area on level ground away from the main seating area. Portable grills can be moved if the wind shifts and blows smoke toward the dinner area. Never, never use an open-air charcoal grill indoors or in an enclosed area without ventilation; fire produces deadly carbon monoxide.

There are many methods of lighting charcoal: the stovepipe method, using an electric starter, or self-starting treated briquettes. The stovepipe method is easy. Place the pipe in the barbecue pan, put several pieces of crumbled newspaper into the pipe, and top with charcoal. Light the paper, and after about fifteen minutes when the charcoal is ash-gray, lift the pipe, and the fire will spread. When using an electric starter or self-starting briquettes, stack the coals in a pyramid before igniting them. If using a liquid starter, give the coals a good dousing, then ignite. Never add more fluid from the can once the fire has started, even if it appears dead. I use about twelve briquettes per pound of meat to be cooked.

For optimum heat, wait until the coals turn ashen gray before you start to cook. Avoid flare-ups by using a grease pan set into the grill directly under the food. For proper cooking of different foods, the grill should be adjustable up and down. Coat the grill with vegetable oil so that the food will not stick. Cook steaks and chops close to the heat, poultry and roasts higher up. Hooded grills offer the advantage of cooking and roasting large cuts like whole turkeys, chickens, or ducks. Even chicken parts and large steaks benefit from this. You can "smoke" combinations of fish and vegetables by using an open foil pack with the lid closed. (Directions appear in the following recipes.)

While the main course is grilling, why not create your own salad bar for your guests. You can invite everyone to help themselves from huge bowls of different greens and a variety of dressings with name tags. Or serve one of the salads suggested here.

BARBECUE SAUCE

Sauces are made to be brushed on meats while they cook, as opposed to marinades, which are usually used before cooking to tenderize and permeate the meat, chicken, or fish. Do not brush barbecue sauces on meats and chicken until after the first 10 minutes of cooking. You will be rewarded when done with a more flavorful product, because the sauce will have a chance to cling better once the meat is hot.

1 teaspoon unsalted butter
1 small onion, chopped
1 teaspoon dark brown sugar
$1/2$ cup dry white wine
1 teaspoon Worcestershire sauce
1 cup ketchup
$1/2$ cup water
1 cup tomato sauce
1 clove garlic, minced
1 bay leaf

Melt the butter in a medium pan. Add the chopped onion and cook until soft, approximately 5 minutes. Add the rest of the ingredients and cook for 5 minutes over low heat. Store the sauce in the refrigerator in a jar with a screw-on cover until needed. *Makes approximately 3 cups.*

BARBECUE MARINADE

Marinate chicken, pork, and lesser cuts of beef in this mixture in the refrigerator for 24 hours before cooking. The marinade permeates the meat and adds a tantalizing taste.

1/4 pound margarine
1/2 cup A-1 steak sauce
1/4 cup Worcestershire sauce
Juice of 1 lemon
1 or 2 dashes of hot pepper sauce
Freshly ground pepper to taste
1/2 cup white wine

Melt the margarine in a saucepan over low heat, and mix in all the other ingredients except the wine. Mix thoroughly, remove from the heat, and add the wine. Place the meat in a bowl, cover with marinade, and refrigerate for 12 to 24 hours before cooking. Discard the marinade, and grill the meat as usual. *Makes approximately 1 1/2 cups.*

FISH KEBABS

You can use frozen fish fillets for this recipe. Thaw them in the refrigerator before grilling.

6 fresh flounder fillets or any similar fish fillets, cut in
　　half lengthwise (1 1/2 to 2 pounds total weight)
3/4 cup dry white wine
1/2 cup olive oil
3 tablespoons fine dry bread crumbs
1/2 teaspoon salt, if desired
1/2 teaspoon marjoram, crushed
2 medium zucchini, cut into 8 thick round slices
12 cherry tomatoes

Wash the fish pieces and pat dry. In a bowl, combine the wine, oil, bread crumbs, salt if desired, and marjoram. Add the fish pieces and coat with the wine mixture. Chill and marinate for at least 30 minutes, or up to 2 hours.

Remove the fish from the marinade, reserving the marinade. Roll up the fish and thread onto six 10-inch skewers, alternating with the zucchini slices and cherry tomatoes. Brush kabobs with marinade.

Grill or broil about 4 inches from heat source for about 10 to 12 minutes. Turn once during the cooking. Fish is done when it flakes when tested with a fork. Serve immediately. *Serves 6.*

STEAMED FISH IN FOIL

Here's an almost foolproof method of putting together an impressive meal while spending time with your guests. Make up the foil packet up to two hours before your guests arrive, store it in the refrigerator, and it will be ready to pop on the grill when it is time to cook.

4 tablespoons olive oil
12 medium shrimp, peeled and deveined
$^1/_2$ pound scallops
12 littleneck clams
$^3/_4$ pound halibut fillet or other fish fillet
1 small head broccoli
2 red or yellow bell peppers
1 carrot
3 large mushrooms
1 bay leaf
Pinch of marjoram
$^1/_4$ teaspoon oregano
$^1/_2$ cup white wine
Juice of $^1/_2$ lemon
Freshly ground pepper to taste
Salt, if desired
Dash of dried hot red pepper flakes, if desired

Coat one side of a large piece of heavy-duty extra-wide aluminum foil with oil. Place all the seafood and fish in the center of the foil.

Wash the broccoli and bell peppers, peel the carrot, and wipe off the mushrooms. Do not shake out any excess water. Cut the vegetables into bite-size pieces and place them on top of the seafood.

Turn up the edges of the foil so that the liquid will not escape, and sprinkle with the bay leaf, marjoram, oregano, wine, lemon juice, and pepper. Add salt and hot pepper flakes if desired. Bring the other half of the foil down over the food and carefully fold the two edges together all the way around so that you have sealed the packet.

Place the packet on the grill and cook for about 20 to 25 minutes, then check to see if the fish is done by carefully opening one side of the foil packet. If your grill has a lid, you can open the top of the foil packet after the first 15 minutes of cooking and finish cooking with the grill hood closed. For gas or electric grills, set the heat to a little above low. When cooked in this manner, the fish will have a barbecue taste. *Serves 6.*

GRILLED LAMB DINNER

This is so simple that it will alleviate a lot of stress you might otherwise feel when you invite friends over for a barbecue. Make the packets up a few hours before your guests arrive and refrigerate.

6 large shoulder lamb chops
$1/2$ cup olive oil
1 tablespoon red-wine vinegar
1 tablespoon grated onion
$1/2$ teaspoon dried rosemary
Salt, if desired
2 medium zucchini, sliced
2 medium ripe tomatoes, sliced

Cut heavy-duty aluminum foil into 6 squares big enough to fit 1 lamb chop on one-half of the square, leaving 1 or 2 inches at the edges for folding.

Place each chop on the center of each foil piece. Mix together the oil, vinegar, onion, rosemary, and salt if desired. Brush each chop with some of the mixture.

Place zucchini and tomato slices on top of the chops, and drizzle the vegetables with the remainder of the mixture.

Fold into individual packets as described in the recipe for Steamed Fish in Foil (page 200). Cook on the grill to desired degree of doneness, about 16 minutes for medium. If your grill has a hood, you can open the top of the packets after the first 10 minutes of cooking and close the hood of the grill; the chops will acquire a barbecue taste. *Serves 6.*

SLICED TOMATOES WITH MOZZARELLA AND BASIL

Take advantage of summer vine-ripened tomatoes and my favorite herb, fresh basil.

3 ripe tomatoes, thinly sliced
A handful of fresh basil leaves
Freshly made mozzarella, thinly sliced
Extra-virgin olive oil
1 tablespoon capers
Freshly ground pepper to taste

Arrange alternate layers of tomatoes, whole basil leaves, and cheese on a serving plate. Drizzle with olive oil, and sprinkle on the capers and top off with a few turns of the pepper mill. *Serves 6.*

JUST A GOOD SALAD

1 head iceberg lettuce
$^1/_2$ fresh lemon
3 large ripe tomatoes
1 seedless cucumber
2 large red onions
$^1/_2$ cup black oil-cured olives
$^1/_2$ teaspoon oregano
Freshly ground pepper to taste
Salt, if desired

Cut the lettuce in half. Run a cut lemon over the slicing knife to help prevent the lettuce from turning brown. Lay half the lettuce on its flat side and cut in thin strips as you would for cole slaw, alternately running lemon over the blade. Repeat with the other half. Dice the tomatoes and the cucumber. Cut the onions in half, lay them on the flat side, and slice very thinly. Slice the olives. Toss all in a large chilled bowl with oregano and fresh pepper, and salt if desired.

Have a few salad dressings on hand so guests can have a choice, or toss with my All-Purpose Vinaigrette Salad Dressing (page 25). *Serves 8 to 10.*

PICNICS IN THE SNOW

Picnics in the snow can be fun. Of course, you want to choose a winter day that is not blustery or so cold that you can't chew. Pick a warm and peaceful day just after a snowfall, when cross-country skiing, walking in the fields, or horseback riding can keep everyone occupied.

Late in the morning while your guests play, pick a flat spot and cover it with a large plastic liner on the snow, then a blanket and a festive tablecloth. Close by, build a fire under a large pot half-filled with the makings for mulled wine. Unpack a big bowl of fresh fruit salad with poppy seed dressing, some Gorgonzola or Havarti cheese, and peasant bread with a large knife thrust into it. Wasn't it Omar Khayyám who said, "A loaf of bread, a jug of wine and thou . . ."?

MULLED WINE

1 apple, peeled and quartered
2 cinnamon sticks
1 tablespoon whole cloves
Zest of 1 lemon
2¼ cups sugar
2 quarts mineral water (8 cups)
3 liters red wine
Optional:
1 cup brandy

GARNISHES:
1 orange, studded with cloves
Cinnamon sticks

Before you leave home, place the apple, cinnamon sticks, cloves, and lemon zest in a cheesecloth bag and tie with long string.

Pour the sugar and water into a large pot and add the cheesecloth bag. Let the mixture come to a boil, reduce heat, then simmer about 10 to 15 minutes. Pull out the cheesecloth bag and discard. Add the wine and brandy and place over low heat. Do not let the wine boil or you will lose all the alcohol. Garnish with the orange and cinnamon sticks. To serve, ladle into hefty mugs. *Makes 24 6-ounce servings.*

FRUIT SALAD

This is a basic fruit salad made with winter fruits, which is particularly good with the following Poppy Seed Dressing.

2 pink grapefruits
2 large naval oranges
2 Granny Smith apples
3 Red Delicious apples
1 small ripe honeydew melon
3 kiwis
1 pound seedless green grapes
1 pound Red Flame seedless grapes
Poppy Seed Dressing (following recipe)

Peel the grapefruits and oranges; section them and cut into bite-size pieces. Core the apples but do not peel; cut into bite-size pieces. Peel and remove the seeds from the melon; cut into bite-size pieces. Peel and slice the kiwis. Separate the grapes.

In a large bowl convenient for carrying, place the fruit and gently toss with Poppy Seed Dressing. *Serves 24.*

POPPY SEED DRESSING

This makes more than enough for the preceding fruit salad. Refrigerate the extra for another use; it keeps well.

$^1/_2$ cup sugar
1 tablespoon salt
1 tablespoon dry mustard
1 cup distilled white vinegar
3 cups olive oil, extra-light olive oil, or safflower oil
1 medium onion, grated
4 teaspoons poppy seeds

Mix the sugar, salt, mustard, and vinegar. Slowly blend in the oil. Add the onions and poppy seeds and refrigerate. If dressing separates, beat steadily for a few minutes. *Makes 4 cups.*

PICNICS BY THE FIRE

You do not always have to cook in the kitchen. Why not cook and serve your meal in front of the family-room fireplace or by a big picture window? If you have an electric buffet pan or a large plug-in wok, you can set it up anywhere and produce meals like a delicious choucroute garni with smoked meats, pasta in cream sauce with Westphalian ham, and all kinds of tasty crisp vegetables dipped in batter, deepfried, and served with a sweet-and-sour sauce, tempura style.

Frosty mugs of beer, goblets of wine, satisfying foods, and conversation before a crackling fire are a few of life's simple pleasures.

CHOUCROUTE GARNI
(Sauerkraut with Meat)

All meat ingredients used in this recipe are fully cooked and smoked.

4 slices Canadian bacon
1 pound small whole onions, peeled
1 pound small whole red potatoes, scrubbed
Two 1-pound cans sauerkraut, drained
1 apple, peeled, cored, and chopped
2 to 2$^{1}/_{2}$ cups white wine
2 bay leaves
$^{1}/_{2}$ teaspoon ground coriander
2 frankfurters, cut in half
2 bratwurst, cut in half
2 knockwurst, cut in half
1 kielbasa ring, cut into chunks
2 smoked loin pork chops, cut in half
Freshly ground pepper to taste

In a large electric wok or plug-in buffet pan, sauté the bacon and onions until the onions are translucent. Add the potatoes, sauerkraut, and apple. Add the wine, bay leaves, and coriander and mix the ingredients together.

Cover the pan. Simmer slowly approximately 30 minutes. Then add all the meats. Cook approximately 1 hour longer. Check the pan occasionally to see if the wine has

evaporated. Add more wine or water, if needed; the choucroute should be moist when finished.

If you prefer to cook the choucroute in the oven, follow
directions in paragraph one, using a Dutch oven. Then cook,
covered, at 350°F. for 45 minutes. Add all the meats. Reduce
the oven temperature to 300°F. and cook another 45 minutes
to 1 hour, checking the pot occasionally to see if wine has
evaporated. Add more wine or water, as needed. The choucroute should be moist when finished. *Serves 4 to 6.*

PENNE WITH WESTPHALIAN HAM

SAUCE:

4 ounces Westphalian ham, cut into strips
1 small onion, diced
3 tablespoons unsalted butter
1/2 cup fresh or frozen peas
1 cup heavy cream
Freshly ground pepper to taste
4 tablespoons grated Parmesan cheese

PASTA:

8 ounces penne cooked al dente

Sauté the ham and onion in butter until the onion is
translucent. Add the peas, cream, and pepper and simmer
until slightly thickened. Add the cheese and mix thoroughly.

Serve over cooked penne or any other of your favorite
pastas. *Serves 4 as an appetizer or, if doubled, serves 4 as a
main course.*

VEGETABLES, TEMPURA STYLE

2 eggs
1 1/3 cups flour
1 teaspoon salt
1 cup flat beer
Oil for deep frying
Zucchini, mushrooms, string beans, broccoli,
   cauliflower, asparagus cut into bite-size pieces

Beat the eggs and mix in 1/3 cup flour and the salt. Add
the beer alternately with the remaining 1 cup flour, beating
continually. The batter should be thin so that it runs off a
spoon easily. Let the batter stand at room temperature for
about 1 hour.

Heat the oil to 375°F. Dip the vegetable pieces into the
batter and let extra batter drip off. Using tongs, fry the vegetables in small batches, and drain on paper towels. Serve
with Sweet-and-Sour Sauce (following recipe). *Makes enough
batter to coat approximately 48 bite-size vegetable pieces.*

SWEET-AND-SOUR SAUCE

I think this is better than store-bought, and it has no preservatives.

1 tablespoon unsalted butter or margarine
3/4 cup pineapple juice
1/4 cup water
1/2 cup cider vinegar
1/4 cup sugar
3 tablespoons dry sherry
1 tablespoon cornstarch
3 tablespoons soy sauce

Melt the butter or margarine in a saucepan and add the pineapple juice, water, vinegar, sugar, and sherry. Bring to a boil over lower heat and cook for 5 minutes. Mix the cornstarch and soy sauce, then add mixture to the simmering liquid. Continue simmering until thick. *Makes 2 cups.*

ROMANTIC SUPPERS

Everything is so right. You have a warm glow inside, having just returned from watching your daughter (or your grand-daughter) in her first school play. Your mind goes back to the caramel apple all over her dress on Easter Sunday, just a few years ago. How quickly time goes by. As you tuck her in that night you count your blessings. Your mood and soul are full of love, and now you're going to sit down and enjoy a very quiet, very cozy, very *romantic* dinner in celebration.

The table is set with your fine cloth, crystal, and china for two. The candles are flickering; you pour the wine. The first dish I have chosen is a great late-night repast, not too heavy—Coconut Honeymoon Shrimp. According to Caribbean folklore, a local bridegroom, anxious to impress his new bride, gave her a drink of coconut and rum, a drink that has become a traditional wedding drink for toasting. Some years ago I experimented with this liquor and created this romantic recipe. Coconut rum is available in most liquor stores.

Remember, after dinner, don't do the dishes, don't break the mood, let the romance continue.

COCONUT HONEYMOON SHRIMP

This is a light dish, perfect before bedtime. Serve with white rice cooked in water seasoned with a dash of tumeric and 2 tablespoons coconut rum. You can add extra flavor to this recipe by soaking the raisins in the 3 tablespoons of rum 30 minutes before cooking. Remove the raisins and use the raisins and rum as directed.

1/2 pound small shrimp
2 scallions, sliced
2 tablespoons unsalted butter
1 tablespoon olive oil
3 tablespoons coconut rum
1/4 cup golden raisins
Dash of allspice

Peel, clean, and devein the shrimp.

Sauté the scallions in the butter and olive oil. Add the rum, raisins, and allspice and cook for 1 or 2 minutes.

Add the shrimp to the pan and cook until just done, about 4 minutes, or until the shrimp turn pink. *Serves 2.*

CHICKEN IN CHAMPAGNE
GINGER SAUCE

We all appreciate the romance of the "bubbly." Cook this recipe with champagne and share the rest of the bottle together. Serve with white rice and Caraway Carrots (page 29).

1 large chicken breast, split, skinned, and boned
2 tablespoons flour
1/4 teaspoon ground dried sage
3/4 teaspoon ground dried ginger
1 1/2 tablespoons butter
1/2 cup champagne
1 cup chicken stock
1/4 teaspoon ground white pepper
Salt, if desired
1 cup watercress

Butterfly each chicken breast half so that you have 4 thin slices; coat with a mixture of the flour, sage, and ginger. In a skillet, brown chicken in the butter for about 4 minutes on each side. Remove to a warm platter. Add the champagne to the skillet and scrape the bottom. Add chicken stock, pepper, and salt if desired. Stir until reduced to less than half its original volume. Arrange chicken portions on each plate and tuck watercress between the slices. Pour sauce over the chicken and serve. *Serves 2.*

FILET MIGNON WITH MARSALA SAUCE

The time for a small, succulent piece of fine meat dressed with tasty Marsala wine is now. Serve with steamed potatoes and asparagus.

2 tablespoons unsalted butter
$^1/_2$ cup plus 1 tablespoon Marsala wine
2 filets mignons, $1^1/_2$ inches thick each
1 cup beef stock
1 cup fresh mushrooms
Freshly ground black pepper
Salt, if desired
Parsley sprigs for garnish

Preheat oven to 325°.

Melt 1 tablespoon butter in large skillet, and add 1 tablespoon of the Marsala. Quickly brown the filets on each side and remove to an oven-proof dish.

Meanwhile, to the skillet, add $^1/_2$ cup of wine and scrape the bottom of pan; add the beef stock and remaining butter. Continue to cook until sauce starts to reduce, approximately 15 minutes. Add the mushrooms, pepper, and salt if desired. Cook the meat in the oven to desired degree of doneness, about 10 to 12 minutes for rare. Cook sauce until thickened, approximately 10 additional minutes.

Ladle a little sauce onto the dinner plates. Place the meat in the center. Mound mushrooms on top of each filet, and garnish with parsley. Serve immediately. *Serves 2.*

THEME PARTIES

Theme parties are fun. We have all been to some sort of occasion where the decorations and food were geared to a festive event and the guests came away with that sense of being part of something special.

Having had the pleasure of cooking at Churchill Downs on national television and as an annual participant in the hoopla of Kentucky Derby fever, I can tell you that the enthusiastic hospitality in Louisville, Kentucky, reaches across the United States. The running of the Derby on the first Saturday in May is party time.

At Derby parties hosts offer traditional Derby dishes like burgoo—a popular Derby stew made of twenty-eight different ingredients—fried chicken, grits (page 220), Derby pies, and Mint Juleps (page 151), and a chance to pick the winner. To add atmosphere, place photographs and cutouts of horses around your party room and buffet table.

Valentine's Day is a traditional "Made for Lovers Only Day," the day I claim is my birthday because it is the day I am most asked to talk about and to cook aphrodisiac food or a conquest dinner. It should be enjoyed by everyone, including teens. Let me explain: respect, friendship, and love should be shared by kids as well as adults. Valentine's Day is a good time to have a class party, a church youth group shindig, or a choose-your-partner-for-the-prom event.

The party time should be planned with dancing, games,

and contests such as "bring the best dessert and win a prize." The prizes can be the latest record album or your school T-shirt.

Whatever you do or plan, the food should be plentiful and fun. Cheese fondue is perfect for kids because they can do it themselves. Serve with soda pop or with one of the nonalcoholic drink and punch suggestions on pages 161–64.

Another of the greatest shows on earth is New Orleans Mardi Gras. Pre-Lenten Mardi Gras parties are perfect times to cook up some Cajun-Creole country-style dishes like Jambalaya (page 222) perfumed with filé-powdered sassafras leaves and herbs. If you have a party supply house nearby, buy fake beads and doubloons to scatter about the tables. Ask guests to wear unusual masks and enter a contest for the best mask. Give New Orleans jazz tapes or a cookbook (hopefully this one) as a prize.

Chinese New Year presents another excuse for a theme party, replete with chopsticks, paper lanterns, and easy-to-prepare Chinese recipes. And don't forget the fortune cookies. Originally called moon cakes, fortune cookies were first baked with messages inside signaling the people to revolt against the intolerable dynasty at the time.

KENTUCKY DERBY GRITS CASSEROLE

When I came up with this recipe to show on TV as a buffet item for Derby Day, my producer was not enthusiastic. "No one likes grits," he said. I think he is wrong, but you be the judge.

2 teaspoons salt
1 ½ cups quick-cooking grits
8 ounces sharp Cheddar cheese
3 eggs
1 bunch scallions
2 tablespoons olive oil
½ cup unsalted butter
3 tablespoons sesame seeds
½ teaspoon paprika
½ teaspoon garlic powder

Preheat the oven to 350°F.

In a pot, bring 6 cups water and the salt to a boil and gradually add the grits, stirring occasionally. Return the water to a boil, then lower the heat to a simmer, stirring occasionally. It should be thick in about 15 minutes.

Meanwhile, prepare the other ingredients. Shred the cheese. Separate the eggs and beat the yolks. Whip the whites until peaks form. Slice the scallions very thin, and mix with 1 tablespoon olive oil.

When the grits are cooked, remove them from the heat; stir in the butter, sesame seeds, cheese, paprika, garlic powder, and egg yolks. Carefully fold in the egg whites. Grease a 7½-by-11¾-inch casserole with the remaining oil. Pour in the mixture.

Bake 30 minutes. Sprinkle on the scallions and cook an

additional 20 to 30 minutes, until firm. *Serves 8 to 10 as a side dish.*

CHEESE FONDUE

Fondues are fun and everyone likes the congeniality of dipping into the same pot. Don't worry if you have given away your fondue pot; take out that old electric Crockpot—it works fine. For a teenage party, make the fondue with cider; for adults, use white wine.

1 clove garlic
3 cups unsweetened apple cider or white wine
$^1/_2$ small onion, chopped
$^1/_2$ red bell pepper, chopped
2 pounds Jarlsberg cheese, shredded
6 tablespoons flour
2 teaspoons dry mustard
1 teaspoon white pepper
$^1/_4$ teaspoon nutmeg
For dipping:
French bread, cut into cubes, or raw vegetables

Rub the garlic around the inside of the fondue pot. Heat the cider or wine, and add the onion and red pepper.

Toss the cheese with the flour, then gradually drizzle it into the hot liquid. Stir until the cheese melts; mix in the mustard. The fondue is ready when it is smooth and thick. Season with pepper and nutmeg. Now spear your choice of bread or vegetable with long wooden cocktail picks or fondue forks, and have fun. *Serves approximately 10 to 12.*

JAMBALAYA

One of the great advantages of this recipe is that it can be cooked ahead of time and reheated, and it is easily doubled.

This version is not overly spicy. Serve Louisiana hot sauce and perhaps some filé powder (available in specialty shops) for guests who would like to increase the heat. Cajun sausage, andouille, is available at specialty meat departments; otherwise, use spicy kielbasa.

3 tablespoons unsalted margarine
$1/4$ pound smoked ham, cubed
$1/2$ pound andouille sausage or kielbasa, chopped
3 cloves garlic, minced
1 large onion, chopped
Two 16-ounce cans stewed tomatoes
1 large green bell pepper, chopped
3 to 4 ribs celery, chopped
2 pounds boneless, skinless chicken, cut in bite-size
    pieces
3 whole bay leaves
$1/2$ teaspoon cayenne pepper
$3/4$ teaspoon dried thyme
2 cups chicken stock
2 cups uncooked white rice
2 pounds small shrimp, peeled and deveined
Salt, if desired

Melt the margarine in a large skillet. Sauté the ham and sausages until crisp, about 6 minutes. Add the garlic and onion and cook an additional 2 minutes.

Add the tomatoes to the skillet with the green pepper, celery, and chicken. Season with bay leaves, cayenne pepper, and thyme. Stir and reduce the heat to a simmer.

Meanwhile, in a separate pan, bring the chicken stock to a boil, add the rice, and cook over medium heat for 5 minutes.

Mix the rice and stock into the main ingredients. Add the shrimp and salt if desired. Cover the skillet and simmer on top of the stove approximately 20 minutes, or until the rice is tender. If there is too much liquid, remove the cover for the last 10 minutes of cooking. *Serves 10 to 12.*

PORK LO MEIN

2 large dried black shiitake mushrooms
1¼ to 1½ pounds lean pork loin
3 scallions
½ cup bamboo shoots
½ pound dried or fresh Oriental noodles
1 tablespoon sesame oil
3 tablespoons vegetable oil
2 cups fresh bean sprouts, soaked in water and
    drained
3 tablespoons sherry
1 tablespoon oyster sauce
2 tablespoons soy sauce

Soak the mushrooms in warm water 30 minutes before you start cooking. Squeeze out the water from the mushrooms. Slice the mushrooms, pork, scallions, and bamboo shoots into thin julienne strips.

Cook the noodles, drain, rinse in cold water, drain again, and toss with the sesame oil. Set aside.

Heat the vegetable oil in a wok or skillet. Stir-fry the pork about 5 minutes until browned, then add the mushrooms. Stir-fry for 1 minute longer. Add the bamboo shoots, scallions, bean sprouts, sherry, and oyster sauce. Mix and stir-fry for 3 minutes more.

Add the cooked noodles to the wok and sprinkle with soy sauce. Mix thoroughly to combine with other ingredients. Stir-fry an additional 4 minutes. *Serves 6.*

X.
Coups de Grâce

❖

Fish Dumplings, Quenelles Style

Ligurian Sautéed Ducklings

Crown Rack of Lamb

Rice and Peas

Rock Cornish Hens in Baker's Clay

Wild Rice Stuffing

Sesame Bay Scallops and Snow Peas

My Mother's Cream Puffs

Peach Soufflé

Peachy Sauce

Peaches Ablaze with Bourbon

❖

COUPS DE GRÂCE

This is the meal with which you "knock 'em dead." This is your declaration that you have mastered the art of cooking. You may have enjoyed some of the recipes here in the fanciest restaurants and now, from the best kitchen in the world—yours—come these *coups de grâce*.

Sometimes on the surface a thing looks difficult and even beyond our reach, but a closer look reveals that it is not as complicated as you thought it might be. Of course you can do it. Look through the ingredients and procedures. They are not at all impossible for someone who has achieved what you have in your kitchen. Yes, they may be showy, but that is what you want; the ohs and ahs when this dish is brought to the table; the recognition that by golly, I am a good cook, I created this, I made this myself. Reading these recipes, the dishes may appear too ambitious, but look again, and relax; they are really not as difficult as you may think. I suggest you attempt only one of these dishes at any given time, until you are more comfortable. Visualize how the final product will look and how you will add your flourishes and touches.

It may be the difference between the usual and the unusual, the difference between mediocre food and inspiring food, or it may be something as simple as an unusual platter you picked up at a flea market last summer. The major difference to your guests will be your individuality. Just sit quietly, uninterrupted; be creative and visualize. Now let's cook.

FISH DUMPLINGS, QUENELLES STYLE

Traditionally, quenelles are poached in a fish stock. If you do not wish to make fish stock, flavor boiling water with a vegetable bouillon cube or cut up an onion, 2 celery stalks, a handful of parsley, and add salt.

1/2 pound scallops
1/2 pound halibut fillets, cut into large pieces
1 egg
1/8 teaspoon white pepper
3 tablespoons dry bread crumbs
5 drops of hot red pepper sauce
Pinch of freshly grated nutmeg
Salt, if desired
1 1/2 cups heavy cream
Fish stock or seasoned water
Pesto Cream Sauce (page 60) or Herbed Sauce (page 98)

Put the scallops and halibut in the bowl of a food processor with the knife blade in place. Add the egg, white pepper, bread crumbs, hot red pepper sauce, nutmeg, and salt if desired, and process for approximately 45 seconds, scraping down the sides, if necessary, halfway through. With the processor running, slowly pour the cream down the feed tube and process until thick and smooth, about 40 seconds.

Cover the food processor bowl with plastic wrap and place in the freezer for about 12 minutes.

Meanwhile, bring fish stock or seasoned water to a boil in a large shallow (12-inch diameter) pan on top of the stove; the liquid should come up to about 1½ inches. Adjust the heat so the liquid maintains a simmer. Place a bowl of hot water next to the stove.

With the aid of 2 tablespoons, scoop the mixture and form dumplings, carefully easing them into the simmering broth. Do not cook more than 12 dumplings at one time, so the broth remains at a constant gentle simmer. Clean the spoons in the bowl of hot water before forming each new dumpling. Poach the dumplings for 12 minutes.

Remove the dumplings from the broth to paper towels with a slotted spoon, and allow them to drain.

To serve with Pesto Cream Sauce, spoon a thick layer of the sauce onto each serving plate, and place the dumplings on top. Or serve on a platter with a small bowl of Herbed Sauce on the side. *Serves 8 to 10 as an appetizer.*

LIGURIAN SAUTÉED DUCKLINGS

A few years back I was asked by a major department store to join a brigade of Italian chefs who came to demonstrate special Italian recipes in the stores. I was the only participating American chef, so I created this recipe with the flavor of Italy for the American kitchen. To be true to the region of Liguria, you would use white olives; I think green olives are fine. A big plus for this recipe is that it can be made up to one hour ahead and reheated.

2 large ducklings (about 4 pounds each)
2 tablespoons olive oil
2 tablespoons unsalted butter
1 medium onion, minced
1 carrot, minced
1 cup dry white wine
2 bay leaves
2 tablespoons chopped fresh parsley
3/4 teaspoon dried thyme
Freshly ground pepper to taste
30 to 36 green olives, pitted and sliced
1 cup chicken stock
1/2 pound fresh mushrooms, sliced
Watercress for garnish

If you buy frozen ducklings, defrost them in the refrigerator. To cut each duckling into 8 pieces, use a large, heavy knife. Cut each duckling in half by cutting lengthwise through the breastbone and backbone. Cut the second joints from the body, and separate the drumsticks from the second joints. Cut off the wings and discard them. Cut the breast halves across into 2 pieces, cutting off and discarding the attached backbone. You will now have 8 pieces from each duckling. If you can find fresh ducklings at a butcher, you can ask him to cut them into pieces for you.

Cut away any excess fat. Wash the pieces and pat them dry.

Place 8 pieces of duckling in a large skillet, skin side down. Cover the pan and cook over low heat without any oil for approximately 15 to 20 minutes. Remove the duckling and discard the rendered fat. Repeat with the other 8 pieces. Remove the duckling and discard the fat.

In the same pan, heat the oil and butter and sauté the minced onion and carrot for about 3 minutes.

Add the wine and scrape the pan to loosen the little browned bits. Return the browned duckling pieces to the pan and add the bay leaves, parsley, thyme, pepper, olives, and stock. Cover the pan and cook for approximately 20 to 30 minutes.

Add the mushrooms to the pan and check the seasoning. You may want to add an additional $1/2$ teaspoon thyme or more pepper. Continue cooking until the duckling is completely cooked, that is when you prick it with a fork and the juices run clear not pink, approximately another 20 minutes. Remove the bay leaves before serving. *Serves 6 to 8.*

CROWN RACK OF LAMB

Ask your favorite butcher to form the crown for you, that is, to create a circle of 2 loins of 8 ribs tied together. Also have him remove the backbone and french the ribs, or scrape off the meat and fat about 2 inches down from the tip of the rib.

One 16-rib crown rack of lamb (about 4¹/₂ to 5¹/₂
   pounds)
Olive oil
Dried sage
Freshly ground pepper to taste
Rice and Peas (following recipe)

Preheat the oven to 350°F.

Brush the meat with olive oil and dust it with sage and pepper. Cover the tips of the bones with aluminum foil to prevent them from burning. Stuff a large ball of aluminum foil in the center of the crown to help keep the shape.

Roast the lamb for 15 minutes in the preheated oven, then reduce the heat to 325°F. and continue to cook until the lamb is blushing pink, a total of about 14 minutes per pound. A 5-pound crown rack needs about 70 minutes to cook, 15 minutes at 350°F. and 55 minutes at 325°F. You can insert a meat thermometer between 2 ribs, being careful not to touch the bones. It should register 130°F. to 135°F. for pink meat, 150°F. for medium.

Remember that meat continues to cook in its own steam

after it is removed from the oven, so you might want to take it out while it is still quite rare.

When the roast is done, remove the foil and fill the crown with the following stuffing of rice and peas. Garnish the bone tips with paper frills or with small whole cooked beets, and place watercress around the rim of the platter. Bring the crown rack to the table for carving. *Serves 6 to 8.*

RICE AND PEAS

This brightly colored dish is an excellent vegetable for company and is also the ideal stuffing for your crown rack of lamb.

1 small onion, diced
4 tablespoons unsalted butter
1 tablespoon chopped Italian parsley
3 cups chicken stock
1 ½ cups uncooked long-grain rice
1 ½ cups frozen peas
6 ounces Parmesan cheese, grated
Freshly ground pepper to taste

Gently sauté the onion in the butter until translucent. Add the parsley, stock, and rice. When the rice is almost cooked, add the peas and cook another 5 minutes. Add the grated Parmesan cheese and pepper and mix well.

Spoon the rice into the center of the roasted crown rack of lamb. *Serves 6 to 8.*

ROCK CORNISH HENS IN BAKER'S CLAY

I am going to tell you how to make individual clay ovens in which to cook a Rock Cornish hen for each guest. Making the clay with food ingredients is kid's play and the result is a safe, impressive presentation. Remember that you will need a hammer or mallet to break the clay and discard before serving.

For extra pizzazz, decorate each finished clay oven with colors of the season or your guests' names or any appropriate message. You can use food-dye paint from a bakery-supply store, but felt-tip markers are fine.

7 1/2 cups flour, plus extra for the rolling board
6 cups cornstarch
6 cups salt
6 to 7 cups water

6 Rock Cornish hens
Wild Rice Stuffing (following recipe)
6 tablespoons olive oil

Preheat oven to 450°F.

In a very large bowl, stir together the flour, cornstarch, and salt. Gradually stir in the water; you may not need all 7 cups. Squeeze the mixture with your hands until you have a large smooth ball.

Divide the "clay" mixture into 6 equal parts and, on a lightly floured surface, roll each ball into an oval shape about 1/2 inch thick.

Wash the hens and pat them dry. Do not salt them. Fill each hen with Wild Rice Stuffing or a stuffing of your choice. Truss the birds and brush them with olive oil.

Place each hen in the center of an oval of clay. Completely wrap the hens with the clay and smooth the seams with moistened fingers.

Place the hens in a shallow baking pan and bake in the oven for 1 hour, or until the clay is browned. Remove from the oven and let stand 10 minutes to cool.

To decorate the clay, you can paint each clay oven with one color, then contrast a name or message on it with another color. For example, for a Fourth of July party, use red, white, and blue as your theme.

Present the decorated clay ovens at the table with appropriate fanfare. Bring them back to the kitchen and wrap a towel around the first hen. Crack the clay with a mallet or hammer and discard the pieces. Place the cooked hen on a platter, and repeat with the other hens. *Serves 6.*

WILD RICE STUFFING

$^1/_2$ pound wild rice
2 cups chicken stock
$^1/_2$ cup dried apricots, cut into pieces
6 slices whole wheat bread, torn into pieces
$^1/_2$ to $^3/_4$ cup milk
1 large onion, finely minced
$^1/_2$ cup chopped hazelnuts or pecans
$^1/_2$ cup unsalted butter
4 tablespoons brandy or Cognac
$^1/_2$ teaspoon white pepper

Cook the rice, covered, in the chicken stock until nearly done, about 30 minutes. Add the cut-up apricots.

Meanwhile, in a large bowl, give the bread a milk bath by pouring the milk over the bread pieces.

Sauté the onion and hazelnuts in the butter until the onion is translucent. Add to the bread along with the cooked rice with apricots and the brandy. Season with pepper, and mix the stuffing with your hands. Loosely stuff the game hens. *Makes enough to stuff 6 hens.*

SESAME BAY SCALLOPS AND SNOW PEAS

This light, cold appetizer is perfect for parties because it can be made a day in advance.

1½ pounds bay scallops (large sea scallops can be substituted, if cut up)
8 ounces snow peas
1 carrot, julienned
2 tablespoons sesame oil
1 teaspoon dried ground coriander
2 tablespoons sesame seeds

GARNISHES:
1 bunch watercress
2 lemons, sliced thin

Quickly sauté scallops, snow peas, and carrot in hot oil for about 3 to 4 minutes. Remove from heat and toss with coriander and sesame seeds. Cover and refrigerate until chilled. When serving, divide watercress onto each plate, arrange scallop mixture, and add a few lemon slices to one side of the plate for garnish. *Serves 6 to 8.*

MY MOTHER'S CREAM PUFFS

Remember biting into a cream doughnut and looking for the cream? Here are really creamy cream puffs, my mother's way. The filling may be made a day ahead of time and kept in the refrigerator.

PUFFS:

    1 cup water
    $1/4$ pound unsalted butter
    Pinch of salt
    1 cup flour
    4 eggs, beaten
    Margarine or oil for greasing the cookie sheet

Preheat the oven to 425°F.

Bring the water to a boil in a medium pot, and melt the butter in it. Add the salt. Dump in the flour all at once, stirring briskly with a wooden spoon. When it is well mixed, remove it from the heat and slowly beat in the eggs until well blended.

Drop by tablespoons (half-teaspoons will give you miniature puffs) onto a greased cookie sheet, being careful not to put them too close together. (Lightly greasing the spoons keeps the dough from sticking.)

Bake the puffs for about 18 minutes, then reduce the heat to 350°F. and continue cooking for about 10 minutes more. Puffs should be golden brown. You can make these up to 8 hours in advance; store in a dry place. *Makes about 3 dozen regular-size puffs or up to 6 dozen mini puffs.*

CREAM FILLING:
    1 ³/₄ cups plus ¹/₂ cup milk
    ¹/₂ cup flour
    ²/₃ cup sugar
    Pinch of salt
    2 eggs, beaten
    1 teaspoon vanilla
    1 teaspoon rum

Scald 1 ³/₄ cups milk to just below the boiling point. Mix the flour with the remaining ¹/₂ cup milk, and add it to the hot milk, stirring constantly. Add the sugar, salt, and beaten eggs and keep stirring until it thickens, about 10 minutes. Add the vanilla and rum and let cool. (If you are out of rum, use 2 teaspoons vanilla.) If you are making the filling ahead of time, refrigerate.

Pipe the filling into the shells with a pastry bag, or slice the shells in half with a new single-edge razor blade and fill with spoonfuls of the cream filling.

PEACH SOUFFLÉ

Make this a couple of times for your afternoon "coffee klatch" and you will be confident and your guests will be impressed.

4 tablespoons unsalted butter
3 tablespoons granulated sugar
$^{1}/_{2}$ cup half-and-half
2 tablespoons flour
1 teaspoon vanilla
3 ounces peach schnapps or your favorite fruit liqueur
5 egg yolks
6 egg whites
$^{1}/_{4}$ teaspoon cream of tartar
Confectioner's sugar for dusting

Using 2 tablespoons butter, grease the inside of a soufflé dish and a rectangular piece of aluminum foil or wax paper large enough to make a collar around the dish that rises 3 inches above the lip. Dust the inside of the dish with 1 tablespoon granulated sugar. Tie the foil or paper around the outside of the soufflé dish, buttered side in.

Heat the half-and-half to scalding, that is, just below the boiling point.

In a saucepan, melt the remaining 2 tablespoons butter, add the flour, and mix well. Whisk in the scalded half-and-half, the vanilla, and peach schnapps. Cook 5 minutes over medium heat, whisking continually. Remove from the heat and set aside.

Preheat the oven to 400°F.

In a large bowl, beat the egg yolks with 1 tablespoon sugar until the yolks double in volume. Whisk the cooled half-and-half mixture into the yolks.

In another bowl, beat the egg whites with the cream of tartar until stiff but still moist; beat in the remaining table-spoon granulated sugar. With a rubber spatula, gently fold the egg whites into the half-and-half and eggs. Carefully spoon the mixture into the prepared soufflé dish; it should come no higher than three-quarters up the side of the dish.

Bake approximately 30 minutes, or until a cake tester put into the center comes out clean. The soufflé is done when it is well puffed and lightly browned. Dust with con-fectioner's sugar and bring to the table immediately. Remove the collar and serve alone or with the following easy sauce. *Serves 6*.

PEACHY SAUCE

2 tablespoons unsalted butter
Two 4 1/4-ounce jars baby-food peaches, or 1 cup
    puréed canned peaches
2 egg yolks, beaten
1 1/2 cups half-and-half
1/2 teaspoon vanilla
1/2 cup peach schnapps

In a large skillet, melt the butter and add the peaches. Mix in the egg yolks and blend in the half-and-half, vanilla, and peach schnapps. Cook over medium heat until thick, about 6 to 8 minutes, stirring continually. Serve warm over the soufflé.

PEACHES ABLAZE WITH BOURBON

This is a great dessert to top off a special meal and can be made at the table in a chafing dish, but don't singe your eyelashes. The bourbon for flaming should be warmed slightly in a small pan ahead of time. (Do not let it boil; the alcohol will evaporate and there will be no flame.)

3 tablespoons unsalted butter
1 tablespoon grated orange peel
$1/4$ cup white or golden raisins
3 to 4 peaches, peeled and cut in half, or 6 to 8
    canned peach halves
2 teaspoons sugar
Juice of $1/2$ lemon
$1/4$ teaspoon pumpkin pie spice
2 to 3 tablespoons orange marmalade
3 ounces bourbon, warmed
1 cup heavy cream, whipped

Melt the butter in a chafing dish or skillet, and add the orange peel and raisins. Cook the peaches for a few minutes in the butter, turning them once. Sprinkle with sugar, lemon juice, and pumpkin pie spice.

When the peaches appear almost golden brown, turn them, cavity side up, and fill each cavity with marmalade.

Drizzle the warmed bourbon onto the peaches and light it. Shake the pan gently to and fro until the flame burns out.

Remove the peaches to individual serving dishes. Quickly stir the sauce to "marry" the ingredients, then spoon it over the peaches. Serve with freshly whipped cream. *Serves 6 to 8.*

GLOSSARY

Blanch To plunge foods briefly into boiling water to set the color and flavor, as for vegetables before freezing; to loosen the skin, as for tomatoes or peaches; or to remove excess salt, as for bacon.

Boil down and reduce To boil a sauce or other liquid until the volume is reduced and the flavor is intensified.

Defat or Degrease To remove the fat from soup, stock, pan juices, sauces, gravy, et cetera. Degreasing is accomplished by removing the fat from the surface of a hot liquid with a spoon; by chilling the liquid until the fat rises to the top and hardens, making removal easier; or by pouring quite a few ice cubes into the hot liquid so that the fat will congeal somewhat and cling to the cubes, which can then be lifted out.

Deglaze To loosen the pan drippings from a roasting pan, skillet, or other vessel used in cooking by heating and stirring in wine, stock, or other liquid.

Dust To sprinkle with sugar, flour, et cetera.

Dutch oven A large heavy pot, often of cast iron, with a tight-fitting lid. Used for stewing, braising, and so forth.

Julienne To cut into long, thin strips.

Mince To cut or chop into small bits.

Omelette pan A pan designed with sloping sides for easy maneuvering so that an omelette can be turned without breaking.

Roux For these recipes, a roux is a mixture of equal parts flour and butter cooked for about 5 minutes and used as a thickening agent.

Sauté To cook quickly in an uncovered pan with a little oil or butter.

Stir-frying The Chinese method of quick-cooking slices and strips of vegetables and meats over high heat in a little oil. Timing and preparation are key factors.

Sweat To cook chopped vegetables in a little fat over low heat until just before any browning occurs.

Truss To fasten by tying or pinning the wings and legs of poultry or game.

Zest The outside colored skin from any citrus fruit.

SOME ODDS AND ENDS

Plastic food bags make great throwaway pastry bags.

Pineapple is a natural meat tenderizer.

I prefer olive oil to other vegetable oils because of its flavor and health benefits. Use extra-virgin olive oil for salad dressings and pure Italian olive oil for cooking. You may like the lighter olive oil, called light or extra-light; it has less olive flavor.

Dijon mustard is my favorite mustard for cooking. It is a unique mustard that originated in Dijon, France, and it is now made in the United States as well. It consists of prepared mustard seasoned with spices, vinegar, and white wine.

Always discard bay leaves before serving.

A piece of celery added to a pan when cooking cabbage and broccoli will eliminate odors. Also, celery tops rubbed on your hands are great for removing garlic, onion, or fish odors.

A little lemon juice added to white rice while boiling will result in whiter rice with well-separated grains.

To remove excess salt from soup, add slices of uncooked potato, boil, then remove.

Adding a touch of cream or milk to beef or poultry gravy

just when you thicken it will make a richer and creamier gravy.

Purchase an instant-reading thermometer, not the regular meat thermometer, for a quick check of internal roasting temperature.

Do not store onions with potatoes because the moisture from the potatoes can cause the onions to sprout.

THE BASICS

3 teaspoons	= 1 tablespoon
2 tablespoons	= 1 ounce
4 tablespoons	= $\frac{1}{4}$ cup
16 tablespoons	= 1 cup
2 cups	= 1 pint
4 cups	= 1 quart
2 cups	= 1 pound granulated sugar
$2\frac{1}{3}$ cups	= 1 pound confectioner's sugar
$\frac{1}{4}$ pound butter	= $\frac{1}{2}$ cup
1 pound all-purpose flour	= 4 cups, sifted

BEEF

Rare	120°–125°F.
Medium	135°–145°F.
Well	150°–160°F.

VEAL

Medium-well	160°F.
	(reaches maximum flavor)

LAMB

Rare	130°–135°F.
Medium	150°–160°F.
Well	170°F.

PORK	170°–185°F.
CHICKEN	190°F.
TURKEY	180°–185°F.
TURKEY (stuffed)	165°F.
	(when thermometer is inserted into stuffing)

INDEX

249

Index

Index

Index

Index

Index

Index

Index

Index